A
GEOGRAPHIC
DICTIONARY
OF
NEW JERSEY

By
HENRY GANNETT

Baltimore
GENEALOGICAL PUBLISHING CO., INC.
1978

Originally published: Washington, D.C., 1894
as U.S. Geological Survey, Bulletin No. 118
Reprinted: Genealogical Publishing Co., Inc.
Baltimore, 1978
From a volume in the George Peabody Branch,
Enoch Pratt Free Library,
Baltimore, Maryland
Library of Congress Catalogue Card Number 78-59122
International Standard Book Number 0-8063-0819-2
Made in the United States of America

UNITED STATES GEOLOGICAL SURVEY

J. W. POWELL, DIRECTOR

A

GEOGRAPHIC DICTIONARY

OF

NEW JERSEY

BY

HENRY GANNETT

WASHINGTON

GOVERNMENT PRINTING OFFICE

1894

LETTER OF TRANSMITTAL.

DEPARTMENT OF THE INTERIOR,
U. S. GEOLOGICAL SURVEY, DIVISION OF GEOGRAPHY,
Washington, D. C., May 20, 1894.

SIR: I have the honor to transmit herewith a geographic dictionary of New Jersey.

Very respectfully,

HENRY GANNETT,
Chief Topographer.

Hon. J. W. POWELL,
Director, U. S. Geological Survey.

5

A GEOGRAPHIC DICTIONARY OF NEW JERSEY.

BY HENRY GANNETT.

The Geographic Dictionary of New Jersey, which constitutes this bulletin, is designed to aid in finding any geographic feature upon the atlas sheets of that State published by the U. S. Geological Survey. It contains all the names given upon those sheets, and no other. Under each name is a brief statement showing the feature it designates and its location, and opposite to it is the name of the atlas sheet, or sheets, upon which it is to be found.

The atlas sheets upon which the State is represented are the result of a survey made in part by the State of New Jersey and in part by the U. S. Geological Survey. The plan of the work, the scale, the contour intervals, the number and variety of the features represented and their mode of representation, and the methods of survey, were designed by the geological survey of New Jersey. About half the area of the State, including the northern part, had been surveyed by that organization when the work was taken up by the U. S. Geological Survey, which carried it forward to completion. Although the southern part of the State was surveyed at the expense of the U. S. Geological Survey, the methods and, in the main, the personnel which had been employed by the State, remained unchanged.

The scale upon which the sheets are published is 1 : 62500; that is, a distance of 62,500 inches upon the ground, or very nearly 1 mile, is represented by 1 inch upon the map. Relief, or the variation of elevation, is represented by contour lines or lines of equal elevation above mean sea level, these contour lines being at vertical intervals of 10 feet in the low and level portions of the State and 20 feet in the more broken portions. Upon the map all water features, that is, lakes, ponds, rivers, etc., are represented in blue; the contour lines representing the relief, together with the figures showing the elevation, are printed in brown; and the lettering and all symbols representing the works of man are printed in black.

The area of the State is represented upon 49 sheets, each sheet, with one or two exceptions, comprising 15 minutes of latitude by 15 minutes of longitude. Each sheet, therefore, includes about 17 miles from north to south and about 13 miles from east to west. Of these sheets, 32 lie entirely within the State, the remaining 17 including adjacent portions of New York, Pennsylvania, and Delaware. The following is a list of the sheets, showing the names assigned to them and their limits in latitude and longitude:

Sheets.	Limits.			
	In latitude.		In longitude.	
	° ′ ° ′		° ′ ° ′	
Tarrytown............	41 00 to	41 15	73 45 to	74 00
Ramapo	41 00	41 15	74 00	74 15
Greenwood Lake	41 00	41 15	74 15	74 30
Franklin	41 00	44 15	74 30	74 45
Wallpack............	41 00	41 15	74 45	75 00
Bushkill Falls........	41 00	41 15	75 00	75 15
Harlem..............	40 45	41 00	73 45	75 00
Paterson	40 45	41 00	74 00	74 15
Morristown	40 45	41 00	74 15	74 30
Lake Hopatcong	40 45	41 00	74 30	74 45
Hackettstown........	40 45	41 00	74 45	75 00
Delaware Water Gap .	40 45	41 00	75 00	75 15
Staten Island	40 30	40 45	74 00	74 15
Plainfield............	40 30	40 45	74 15	74 30
Somerville...........	40 30	40 45	74 30	74 45
High Bridge.........	40 30	40 45	74 45	75 00
Easton	40 30	40 45	75 00	75 15
Sandy Hook	40 15	40 30	74 00	74 15
New Brunswick	40 15	40 30	74 15	74 30
Princeton............	40 15	40 30	74 30	74 45
Lambertville........	40 15	40 30	74 45	75 00
Doylestown	40 15	40 30	75 00	75 15
Asbury Park	40 00	40 15	74 00	74 15
Cassville	40 00	40 15	74 15	74 30
Bordentown	40 00	40 15	74 30	74 45
Burlington...........	40 00	40 15	74 45	75 00
Germantown.........	40 00	40 15	75 00	75 15
Barnegat............	39 45	40 00	74 00	74 15
Whiting	39 45	40 00	74 15	74 30
Pemberton	39 45	40 00	74 30	74 45
Mount Holly	39 45	40 00	74 45	75 00
Philadelphia	39 45	40 00	75 00	75 15
Long Beach..........	39 30	39 45	74 00	74 15
Little Egg Harbor....	39 30	39 45	74 15	74 30
Mullica	39 30	39 45	74 30	74 45
Hammonton	39 30	39 45	74 45	75 00
Glassboro...........	39 30	39 45	75 00	75 15
Salem	39 30	39 45	75 15	75 30
Wilmington..........	39 30	39 45	75 30	75 45
Atlantic City	39 15	39 30	74 15	74 30
Great Egg Harbor....	39 15	39 30	74 30	74 45
Tuckahoe............	39 15	39 30	74 45	75 00

Sheets.	Limits.			
	In latitude.		In longitude.	
	° ′ ° ′		° ′ ° ′	
Bridgeton	39 15 to 39 30		75 00 to 75 15	
Bayside	39 15	39 30	75 15	75 30
Smyrna	39 15	39 30	75 30	75 45
Sea Isle	39 00	39 15	74 30	74 45
Dennisville	39 00	39 15	74 45	75 00
Maurice Cove	39 00	39 15	75 00	75 15
Cape May	38 45	39 00	74 45	75 00

New Jersey is one of the original 13 States; it adopted the Constitution on December 18, 1787.

The boundary line between New Jersey and New York is theoretically an arc of a great circle running from the point of junction of Navesink River with Delaware River to a rock on the west side of Hudson River in latitude 41°. This line as run conforms closely to the statute. The boundary between New Jersey and Pennsylvania is the main channel of the Delaware River.

The total area of New Jersey is, excluding the waters of Delaware Bay, 7,815 square miles. Of this an area estimated at 290 square miles is water surface, leaving as the land surface of the State 7,525 square miles. Of the land surface, 43 per cent is in forests and 6 per cent in tide marsh, leaving a trifle over one-half as cleared land.

The State contains 21 counties, which, with their land areas, are as follows:

County.	Square miles.
Atlantic	567
Bergen	236
Burlington	869
Camden	222
Cape May	256
Cumberland	511
Essex	127
Gloucester	326
Hudson	43
Hunterdon	437
Mercer	226
Middlesex	312
Monmouth	479
Morris	475
Ocean	583
Passaic	198
Salem	359
Somerset	305
Sussex	529
Union	103
Warren	362

A GEOGRAPHIC DICTIONARY OF NEW JERSEY.

Names of sheets.

Abbot; creek in Fairfield Township, Cumberland County, tributary to Back Creek............................... Bayside.

Absecon; light-house on coast of Egg Harbor Township, Atlantic County............................... Atlantic City.

Absecon; life-saving station on Absecon Beach............... Atlantic City.

Absecon; inlet on coast reef on boundary between Galloway and Egg Harbor townships, Atlantic County............... Atlantic City.

Absecon; bay in coast swamp of Galloway and Egg Harbor townships, Atlantic County............................... Atlantic City.

Absecon; creek rising in south part of Galloway Township, ⎰ Atlantic City.
Atlantic County, flowing southeast into Absecon Bay. ⎱ Great Egg Harbor.

Absecon; beach on coast of Egg Harbor Township, Atlantic ⎰ Great Egg Harbor.
County. ⎱ Atlantic City.

Absecon; town in north part of Egg Harbor Township, Atlantic County, in Absecon Creek....................... Great Egg Harbor.

Acquackanonck; township in Passaic County; area, 11 square miles .... Paterson.

Acton; village in Mannington Township, Salem County, on West Jersey R. R... Salem.

Africa; village in Manalapan Township, Monmouth County. Cassville.

Afton; village in north part of Chatham Township, Morris County .... Morristown.

Albertson; brook in Waterford Township, Camden County, ⎰
and Hammonton Township, Atlantic County, tributary ⎱ Hammonton.
to Nescochaque Creek. ⎱ Mullica.

Albion; village in Gloucester Township, Camden County, on Philadelphia and Atlantic R. R............................. Mount Holly.

Aldine; village in Alloway Township, Salem County......... Salem.

Alexandria; township in Hunterdon County; area, 27 square ⎰ High bridge.
miles. ⎱ Easton.

Alexsocken; creek tributary to Delaware River; rises in Delaware Township and forms partial boundary between Delaware and West Amwell townships, Hunterdon County. Lambertville.

Allaire; village in Wall Township, Monmouth County, on Freehold and Jamesburg R. R........................'.... Asbury Park.

Allamuchy; township in Warren County; area, 21 square miles .... Hackettstown.

Allamuchy; village in east central part of Allamuchy Township, Warren County....................................... Hackettstown.

Allamuchy; station on Lehigh and Hudson River R. R., in Allamuchy Township, Warren County..................... Hackettstown.

Allamuchy; pond in central part of Allamuchy Township, Warren County... Hackettstown.

11

12   A GEOGRAPHIC DICTIONARY OF NEW JERSEY.

Names of sheets.

Allen; village in East Windsor Township, Mercer County, on Amboy Division, Pennsylvania R. R............... Bordentown.

Allendale; village in western part of Orvil Township, Bergen County, on New York, Lake Erie and Western R. R....... Ramapo.

Allentown; village in Upper Freehold Township, Monmouth County... Bordentown.

Allenwood; village in Wall Township, Monmouth County, on Freehold and Jamesburg R. R....................... Asbury Park.

Allerville; village in western part of Clinton Township, Hunterdon County .... High Bridge.

Alligator, The; village in Jackson Township, Ocean County. Cassville.

Allimatona; falls in Lamington River, at the point where Morris, Hunterdon, and Somerset counties join............ Somerville.

Alloway; township in Salem County; area, 34 square miles. { Glassboro. Salem.

Alloway; station in Alloway Township, Salem County, on West Jersey R. R.. Salem.

Alloway; village in Alloway Township, Salem County ...... Salem.

Alloway; creek rising in Upper Pittsgrove Township, Salem County, flows southwest through Salem County into Delaware River .... Salem.

Almonesson; village in east part of Deptford Township, Gloucester County.. Philadelphia.

Almonesson; creek in Deptford Township, Gloucester County; tributary to Big Timber Creek.................. Philadelphia.

Alpine; village in southeastern part of Harrington Township, Bergen County .... Harlem.

Alquatka Branch; brook in Evesham and Medford townships, Burlington County, flows into Mullica River............. Mount Holly.

Ambrose; brook in Raritan and Piscataway townships, Mid- { Plainfield. dlesex County; tributary to Raritan River. { Somerville.

Amsterdam; village in western part of Holland Township, Hunterdon County....................................... Easton.

Amwell; village in eastern part of East Amwell Township, Hunterdon County...................................... Lambertville.

Anchoring; islands in New Inlet in Little Egg Harbor Township, Burlington County .... Little Egg Harbor.

Ancora; village in Winslow Township, Camden County, on Camden and Atlantic R. R .... Hammonton.

Anderson; village in southern part of Mansfield Township, Warren County .... Hackettstown.

Andover; township in Sussex County; area, 25 square miles { Wallpack. Hackettstown. Lake Hopatcong. Franklin.

Andover; village in southern part of Andover Township, Sussex County, on Sussex R. R.............................. Lake Hoptacong.

Andover; village in Winslow Township, Camden County, on Philadelphia and Reading R. R............................ Hammonton.

Anglesea; borough on southeast coast of Cape May County. Dennisville.

Anglesea Junction; village in Middle Township, Cape May County, at junction of Anglesea and West Jersey railroads... Dennisville.

Annandale; village in northwest part of Clinton Township, Hunterdon County, on Central R. R. of New Jersey ...... High Bridge.

Names of sheets.

Annaricken; brook in Springfield Township, Burlington
County; flows into Assicunk Creek........................ Bordentown.

Anthonystown; village in Eatontown Township, Monmouth
County .... Sandy Hook.

Apple Pie; hill in Woodland Township, Burlington County;
elevation, 208 feet .... Pemberton.

Applegate; cove projecting from Barnegat Bay into Dover
Township, Ocean County .... Barnegat.

Apgars Corner; village in southern part of Tewksbury Township, Hunterdon County .... High Bridge.

Archertown; village in Plumstead Township, Ocean County. Cassville.

Arcola; village in eastern part of Saddle River Township,
Bergen County... Paterson.

Arlington; village in northwestern part of Kearney Township, Hudson County, on Passaic River and on Orange
Branch of New York and Greenwood Lake R. R........... Paterson.

Arney Mount; village in Springfield Township, Burlington
County.. Bordentown.

Arneytown; village in New Hanover Township, Burlington
County... Bordentown.

Arnold; point projecting from Lower Alloways Creek Township, Salem County, into Delaware River.................. Bayside.

Arnold Branch; brook in Bass River Township, Burlington { Little Egg Harbor.
County, flows into Wading River. { Mullica.

Asbury; village in southeastern part of Franklin Township,
Warren County, and extending over into Bethlehem Township, Hunterdon County, on Musconetcong River......... Easton.

Asbury; station on West Jersey R. R., in Woolwich Township, Gloucester County...................................... Chester.

Asbury Park; borough and summer resort in Monmouth
County, on New York and Long Branch R. R. .... Asbury Park.

Ash; swamp in south part of Fanwood Township, Union
County .... Plainfield.

Ash Lane Station; village in Delaware Township, Camden
County, on Camden and Atlantic R. R..................... Philadelphia.

Aserdaten; village in Lacey Township, Ocean County...... Whitings.

Assanpink; creek rising in Monmouth County, flows through { Bordentown.
Mercer County, and enters Delaware River at Trenton. { Princeton.

Assiscunk; creek flowing northwest across Burlington County
into Delaware River.. Burlington.

Asylum; station in Ewing Township, Mercer County, on Belvidere division, Pennsylvania R. R.......................... Burlington.

Asylum Station; village in central part of Ewing Township,
Mercer County, on Trenton branch of New York Division,
Philadelphia and Reading R. R.............................. Lambertville.

Atco; village in Waterford Township, Camden County, on
Camden and Atlantic R. R................................... Mount Holly.

Athenia; village in central part of Acquackanonck Township,
Passaic County, on Boonton branch of Delaware and
Western R. R., and on Paterson and Newark branch of
New York, Lake Erie, and Western R. R................... Paterson.

Atlantic; township in Monmouth County; area, 32 square
miles .... Sandy Hook.

Names of sheets.

Atlantic; county in southeastern part of New Jersey; area, 613 square miles.
{ Hammonton.
Tuckahoe.
Mullica.
Great Egg Harbor.
Little Egg Harbor.
Atlantic City.

Atlantic; city on the coast of Egg Harbor Township, Atlantic County...... .... Atlantic City.

Atlantic City; life-saving station at Atlantic City .... Atlantic City.

Atlantic Highlands; village in Middletown Township, Monmouth County, on Atlantic Highlands branch of New Jersey Southern R. R .... Sandy Hook.

Atsion: village in Shamong Township, Burlington County, on Mullica River and on New Jersey Southern R. R....... Mullica.

Auburn; village in Oldmans Township, Salem County ...... Salem.

Augusta; village in southern part of Frankford Township, Sussex County, on Paulins Kill and on Sussex R. R ...... Franklin.

Aura; village in Clayton Township, Gloucester County..... Glassboro.

Avalon; village in Middle Township, Cape May County .... Sea Isle.

Avenel; village in central part of Woodbridge Township, Middlesex County, on Perth Amboy branch Pennsylvania R. R.. Plainfield.

Avis Mills; village in Pilesgrove Township, Salem County.. Salem.

Avon Park; village in northeastern part of Piscataway Township, Middlesex County............................ Plainfield.

Avondale; village in Franklin Township, Essex County, on Paterson·and Newark branch of New York, Lake Erie and Western R. R .... Paterson.

Babcock; creek rising in Galloway Township, Atlantic County, flows southwest across Hamilton Township in same county into Great Egg Harbor River.
{ Mullica.
Great Egg Harbor.

Back; creek rising in Fairfield Township, flows south, forming boundary between Fairfield and Lawrence townships, Cumberland County, into Delaware River............... Bayside.

Back; brook in East Amwell Township, Hunterdon County, tributary to Neshanic River............................. Lambertville.

Back Neck; peninsula in coast swamp in Fairfield Township, Cumberland County .... Bayside.

Back Run; stream in Upper Township, Cape May County, tributary to Tuckahoe River .... Tuckahoe.

Back Thorofare; passage in coast swamp in Upper Township, Cape May County...................................... Great Egg Harbor.

Bacon Neck; peninsula in coast swamp in Greenwich Township, Cumberland County.................................. Bayside.

Bacon Run; brook on boundary between Chesterfield and Mansfield townships, Burlington County, tributary to Black Creek.. ...... Bordentown.

Bailey Corners; village in Wall Township, Monmouth County .... Asbury Park.

Baileytown; village in Commercial Township, Cumberland County .... Bridgeton.

Baker Basin; village in Lawrence Township, Mercer County, on Delaware and Raritan Canal .... Princeton.

Bakersville; village in Egg Harbor Township, Atlantic County, on West Jersey R. R.............................. Great Egg Harbor.

Names of sheets.

Baldwin; brook in Hopewell Township, Mercer County, tributary to Stony Brook .... Lambertville.

Balesville; village in eastern part of Hampton Township, Sussex County, on Paulins Kill............................ Wallpack.

Ballanger; creek rising in Little Egg Harbor Township, Burlington County, flows southwest on boundary between Little Egg Harbor and Bass River townships, into Mullica River... Little Egg Harbor.

Ballinger Mill; village in Medford Township, Burlington County .... Mount Holly.

Bamber; village in Lacey Township, Ocean County......... Whitings.

Banard; station in Buena Vista Township, Atlantic County, on Philadelphia and Reading R. R......................... Hammonton.

Bank; creek in north part of Upper Township, Cape May County, tributary to Hughes Creek .... Great Egg Harbor.

Baptisttown; village in northern part of Kingswood Township, Hunterdon County .... Easton.

Barbertown; village in central part of Kingswood Township, Hunterdon County.. Doylestown.

Barckley; brook in Marlboro Township, Monmouth County, and Madison Township, Middlesex County, flows into Matchaponix Brook... New Brunswick.

Bard Branch; brook in Shamong Township, Burlington County, tributary to Springer Creek .... Pemberton.

Bargaintown; village in Central part of Egg Harbor Township, Atlantic County, on Patcong Creek .... Great Egg Harbor.

Barker; brook in Springfield and Easthampton townships, { Bordentown.
Burlington County, flows into Assiscunk Creek. { Burlington.

Barley Sheaf; village in southwestern part of Readington Township, Hunterdon County............................... High Bridge.

Barnegat; village in Union Township, Ocean County, on Tuckerton and New Jersey Southern R. R .... Barnegat.

Barnegat; city on coast of Ocean Township, Ocean County. Barnegat.

Barnegat; inlet projecting from Atlantic Ocean into Ocean Township, Ocean County .... Barnegat.

Barnegat; life-saving station on coast of Ocean Township, Ocean County... Barnegat.

Barnegat; light-house on coast of Ocean Township, Ocean County .... Barnegat.

Barnegat Park; village in Berkeley Township, Ocean County. Barnegat.

Barnegat Pier; point on coast of Berkeley Township, Ocean County .... Barnegat.

Barnsboro; village in Mantua Township, Gloucester County. Philadelphia.

Barrel; islands in Little Egg Harbor, in Little Egg Harbor Township, Burlington County............................... Little Egg Harbor.

Barrentown; village in Atlantic Township, Monmouth County .... Sandy Hook.

Barret Run; brook in Hopewell Township, Cumberland (Bayside.
County, flows into Cohansey Creek. { Bridgeton.

Bartley; village in southern part of Mount Olive Township, Morris County, on High Bridge branch of Central R. R. of New Jersey... Lake Hopatcong.

Barton Run; brook in Waterford Township, Camden County, and Evesham and Medford townships, Burlington County, flows into southwest branch of Rancocas Creek.......... Mount Holly.

Names of sheets.

Basking Ridge; village in eastern part of Bernard Township, Somerset County, on Passaic and Delaware branch of Delaware, Lackawanna and Western R. R .... Somerville.

Bass; river heading in two branches, the East branch and West branch, in Bass River Township, Burlington County, flows into Mullica River.............................. Little Egg Harbor.

Bass River; village in Bass River Township, Burlington County .... Little Egg Harbor.

Bass River; township in Burlington County; area, 80 square miles. ⎰ Mullica.
⎱ Whitings.
⎰ Little Egg Harbor.

Battentown; village in Woolwich Township, Gloucester County, on West Jersey R. R .... Salem.

Batsto; river in Woodland, Shamong, and Washington townships, Burlington County, tributary to Mullica River.... Pemberton.

Batsto; village in Washington Township, Burlington County, on Batsto River.. Mullica.

Bay Head; village in Brick Township, Ocean County, on Philadelphia and Long Branch R. R...................... Asbury Park.

Bay Head; life-saving station on reef in Brick Township, Ocean County .... Asbury Park.

Bay Shore; life-saving station on southwest shore of Lower Township, Cape May County .... Cape May.

Bayside; beacon on coast of Middletown Township, Monmouth County... Sandy Hook.

Bayside; village in Greenwich Township, Cumberland County, on New Jersey Southern R. R.................... Bayside.

Bayonne; city in Hudson County; area, 12 square miles..... Staten Island.

Bayview Avenue; seacoast village in Middletown Township, Monmouth County.. Sandy Hook.

Bayville; village in Berkeley Township, Ocean County...... Barnegat.

Bayway; village in Elizabeth City, Union County, where Baltimore and New York R. R. crosses New York and Long Branch R. R... Staten Island.

Beach; creek in northeast part of Dennis Township, Cape May County, flowing southwest into Ludlam Thorofare. ...... Sea Isle.

Beach; creek in southeast part of Middle Township, Cape May County, flows north into Hereford Inlet............ Dennisville.

Beach Creek; passage in coast swamp in Upper Township, Cape May County. .... Sea Isle.

Beach Glen; village in central part of Rockaway Township, on Hibernia Brook and Hibernia Mine R. R., Morris County .... Morristown.

Beach Haven; village on beach in Englewood Township, Ocean County, on Long Beach R. R....................... Long Beach.

Beach Thorofare; passage in coast swamp in Egg Harbor Township, Atlantic County. ⎰ Atlantic City.
⎱ Great Egg Harbor.

Beacon; hill among Mount Pleasant Hills, in Marlboro Township, Monmouth County; elevation, 386 feet.............. Sandy Hook.

Beacon; hill in Brick Township, Ocean County; elevation, 138 feet. .... Asbury Park.

Beacon; creek in Downe Township, Cumberland County, flows into Delaware River................................ Bridgeton.

Beadon; point projecting from Downe Township, Cumberland County, into Delaware Bay .... Maurice Cove.

Names of sheets.

Bear; book rising in East Windsor Township, flows northwest into Millstone River, in north part of West Windsor Township, Mercer County. .... Princeton.

Bear; brook in Orvil and Washington Townships, Bergen County, tributary to Pascack Creek .... Ramapo.

Bear; creek rising in Stillwater and Green townships, Sussex County, it flows southwest into Warren County, entering Pequest River. { Wallpack. { Hackettstown.

Bear; islands in Manahawken Bay, in Stafford Township, Ocean County .... Long Beach.

Bear; two small ponds in eastern part of Byram Township, Sussex County.. Lake Hopatcong.

Bear; swamp in Downe Township, Cumberland County..... Bridgeton.

Bear; swamp in northwest part of West Windsor Township, Mercer County, along Duck Pond Run .... Princeton.

Bear; swamp in Southampton and Medford townships, Burlington County. { Pemberton. { Mount Holly.

Bear; swamp in northern part of Hampton Township, extending over the boundary into Frankford Township, Sussex County .... Wallpack.

Bear Branch; brook in Landis Township, Cumberland County .... Tuckahoe.

Bear Swamp; creek in Lawrence Township, Cumberland County, flows into Back Creek. { Bridgeton. { Bayside.

Bear Swamp; hill in Randolph Township, Burlington County; elevation, 165 feet .... Whitings.

Bear Swamp; river in Southampton Township, Burlington County, tributary to Little Creek. { Pemberton. { Mount Holly.

Bear Swamp; brook in Howell Township, Monmouth County, flows into Manasquan River .... Asbury Park.

Bear's Head Branch; brook in Landis Township, Cumberland County, flows into Manumuskin River............... Tuckahoe.

Bearport; mountain range extending through West Milford Township, Passaic County, into Orange County, N. Y.... Greenwood Lake.

Beattystown; village in eastern part of Mansfield Township, Warren County, on Musconetcong River.................. Hackettstown.

Beaver; brook in Center Township, Camden County, tributary to Big Timber Creek .... Philadelphia.

Beaver; brook in Warren County, tributary to Pequest River { Hackettstown. { Delaware Water Gap.

Beaver; brook in Morris County, tributary to Rockaway River... Morristown.

Beaver; brook in Morris County, tributary to Weldon Brook. Lake Hopatcong.

Beaver; creek in Oldmans Township, Salem County, flows into Delaware River .... Salem.

Beaver Branch; brook in Maurice River Township, Cumberland County, tributary to Clear Run ..,.................... Tuckahoe.

Beaver Branch; brook in Burlington County; tributary to Wading River. { Little Egg Harbor. { Mullica.

Beaverdam; village in Downe Township, Cumberland County. Bridgeton.

Beaverdam; brook in East Brunswick Township, Middlesex County, tributary to Lawrence Brook. .... New Brunswick.

Beaverdam; river in Southampton Township, Burlington County. { Pemberton. { Mount Holly.

Bull. 118——2

Names of sheets.

Beaver Run; village in northwest part of Hardiston Township, Sussex County .... Franklin.

Beaverville; village in Southampton Township, Burlington County, on Beaverdam River............................ Pemberton.

Beden; brook rising in Hopewell Township, Mercer County, flows through Montgomery Township, Somerset County, into Millstone River. } Princeton. Lambertville.

Bedminster; village in eastern part of Bedminster Township, Somerset County, on north branch of Raritan River...... Somerville.

Bedminster; township in Somerset County; area, 27 square miles .... Somerville.

Bee; branch of Mantua Creek in Washington Township, Gloucester County...................................... Philadelphia.

Beebe Run; brook in Hopewell Township, Cumberland County, flows into Cohansey Creek...................... Bayside.

Beemerville; village in southwestern part of Wantage Township, Sussex County .... Franklin.

Beesley; point projecting into Great Egg Harbor in Upper Township, Cape May County .... Great Egg Harbor.

Beideman Station; village in Stockton Township, Camden County, on Pennsylvania R. R .... Philadelphia.

Belle Mead; village in north part of Montgomery Township, Somerset County, on Philadelphia and Reading R. R.... Princeton.

Belleplain; village in Maurice River Township, Cumberland County, on West Jersey R. R.............................. Tuckahoe.

Belleville; township in Essex County; area, 3 square miles.. Paterson.

Belleville; city in Belleville Township, Essex County, at junction of Second River with Passaic River, and on Paterson and Newark Branch of New York, Lake Erie and Western R. R.. Paterson.

Bellman; creek in Ridgefield Township, Bergen County, tributary to Hackensack River. { Paterson. Harlem.

Belvidere; town, capital of Warren County, is on Delaware River, at mouth of Pequest River, on Belvidere Division of Pennsylvania R. R. and on Lehigh and Hudson River R. R.. Delaware Water Gap.

Ben Davis; point projecting from Pier Point Neck, in Fairfield Township, Cumberland County, into Delaware River. Bayside.

Ben Elder; creek in Upper Township, Cape May County, flows into Peck Bay .... Great Egg Harbor.

Ben Hands Thorofare; passage in coast swamp in Upper Township, Cape May County .... Sea Isle.

Bennett; village in central part of Lower Township, Cape May County, on West Jersey R. R .... Cape May.

Bennett Mill; village in Maurice River Township, Cumberland County .... Tuckahoe.

Bennett Mills; village in Jackson Township, Ocean County, on Meterdeconk River .... Cassville.

Bergen; county in northeast part of the State; area, 245 square miles. { Morristown. Greenwood Lake. Ramapo. Paterson. Harlem. Tarrytown.

Names of sheets.

Bergen; southern point of Bayonne City on Kill Van Kull and Newark Bay... Staten Island.

Bergen Fields; village in Palisade Township, Bergen County, on West Shore R. R...................................... Harlem.

Bergen Mills; village in Millstone Township, Monmouth County, on Millstone River .... New Brunswick.

Berkeley; township in Ocean County; area, 59 square miles. { Whitings. Asbury Park. Barnegat.

Berkeley; village in East Greenwich Township, Gloucester County, on West Jersey R. R. and on Mantua Creek..... Philadelphia.

Berkeley Heights; village in New Providence Township, Union County, on Passaic River and on Passaic and Delaware R. R .... Plainfield.

Berkshire Valley; village in Jefferson Township, Morris County, on Rockaway River.............................. Lake Hopatcong.

Berlin; village in Winslow Township, Camden County, on Camden and Atlantic R. R............................ Mount Holly.

Bernard; township in Somerset County; area, 41 square { Lake Hopatcong. miles. Somerville.

Bernardsville ; village in Bernard Township, Somerset County, at east end of Passaic and Delaware Branch of Delaware, Lackawanna and Western R. R............... Somerville.

Berry; creek rising in Lodi Township, flows through Boiling Springs Township, and empties into Hackensack River in Union Township, Bergen County....................... Paterson.

Berry Chapel; village in Quinton Township, Salem County. Salem.

Berryland; village in Monroe Township, Gloucester County.. Hammonton.

Berryman Run; brook in Landis and Millville Townships, { Bridgeton. Cumberland County, flows into Manantico Creek. Tuckahoe.

Bertrand; island off northern coast of Roxbury Township, Morris County, in Lake Hopatcong....................... Lake Hopatcong.

Bethany Hole Run; brook in Evesham and Medford Townships, Burlington County, tributary to Haynes Creek.... Mount Holly.

Bethel; village in Egg Harbor Township, Atlantic County, on West Jersey R. R....................................... Great Egg Harbor.

Bethel; village in Howell Township, Monmouth County.... Asbury Park.

Bethel; run in Washington Township, Gloucester County, tributary to Mantua Creek.............................. Philadelphia.

Bethel; village in Stockton Township, Camden County..... Philadelphia.

Bethlehem; township in Hunterdon County; area, 24 square { Easton. miles. High Bridge.

Bevans; post-office of Peters Valley, in western part of Sandyston Township, Sussex County............................. Wallpack.

Beverly; village in Beverly Township, Burlington County, on Delaware River and on Amboy Division, Pennsylvania R. R. Burlington.

Beverly; township in Burlington County; area, 6 square miles. Burlington.

Biddle Branch; brook in Woodland Township, Burlington County, tributary to Shoal Branch........................ Whitings.

Big; brook in Marlboro and Atlantic Townships, Monmouth County, tributary to Hop Brook............................ Sandy Hook.

Big; cove, an arm of Lake Hopatcong, indenting the western coast of Roxbury and Jefferson Townships, Morris County. Lake Hopatcong.

Big Bridge Branch; brook in Monroe Township, Gloucester County, flows into Great Egg Harbor River.............. Hammonton.

Names of sheets.

Big Flat; brook in Sandyston Township, Sussex County, eastern tributary to Flat Brook... Wallpack.

Big Mannington Hill; village in Mannington Township, Salem County.. Salem.

Big Neal Branch; brook in Landis Township, Cumberland County, tributary to Manumuskin River................... Tuckahoe.

Big Spring; small pond in northeastern part of Green Township, Sussex County .... Wallpack.

Big Timber; creek rising in Camden and Gloucester counties. It flows northwest, forming boundary between them, into Delaware River at Gloucester City. { Mount Holly. Philadelphia. Glassboro.

Big Wrangel Branch; brook in Manchester Township, Ocean County, tributary to Wrangel Brook .... Whitings.

Billingsport; village in Greenwich Township, Gloucester County, on Delaware River................................ Philadelphia.

Birmingham; village in Pemberton Township, Burlington County, on Philadelphia and Long Branch R. R........... Pemberton.

Birmingham; village in Ewing Township, Mercer County, on New York Division of Philadelphia and Reading R. R. Lambertville.

Bishop Run; brook in Stow Creek Township, Cumberland County, flows into Horse Run............................. Bayside.

Black; brook rising in Chatham Township, flows northeast into Whippany River in south part of Hanover Township, Morris County... Morristown.

Black; brook in Bethlehem and Union townships, Hunterdon County, tributary to Mulhockaway Creek............ High Bridge.

Black; brook in Chatham and Passaic townships, Morris County, tributary to Passaic River. { Plainfield. Somerville.

Black; creek in New Hanover, Chesterfield, and Bordentown townships; flows into Delaware River .... Bordentown.

Black; meadows in Hanover and Chatham townships, Morris County... Morristown.

Black; river in Morris County, forming the headwaters of Lamington River. { Lake Hopatcong. Somerville.

Black Branch; brook in Jackson and Manchester townships, Ocean County, flows into Union Branch of Toms River... Cassville.

Black Mills; village in Manalapan Township, Monmouth County. { Princeton. New Brunswick.

Black Mills; village in Manalapan Township, Monmouth County .... Cassville.

Black Tom; island off Jersey City in New York Upper Bay.. Staten Island.

Blackberry; creek in Eatontown Township, Monmouth County, flows into Pleasure Bay........................... Sandy Hook.

Blackman; swampy island in east part of Upper Township, Cape May County... Sea Isle.

Blackman Branch; brook in Egg Harbor Township, Atlantic County, tributary to Mill Branch of Patcong Creek. Great Egg Harbor.

Blackwater Branch; brook in Landis Township, Cumberland County, flows into Maurice River...................... Glassboro.

Blackwood; village in Gloucester Township, Camden County, on South Branch of Timber Creek .... Philadelphia.

Blair; creek in Stillwater Township, Sussex County, and Hardwick and Blairstown Townships, Warren County, flows into Paulins Kill. { Wallpack. Hackettstown.

Names of sheets.

Blairstown; township in Warren County; area, 32 square miles.

{ Wallpack.
Bushkill Falls.
Delaware Water Gap.
Hackettstown.

Blairstown; village in eastern part of Blairstown Township, Warren County, on Paulins Kill, and on New York, Susquehanna and Western R. R.............................. Hackettstown.

Bloomfield; township in Essex County; area, 7 square miles. Paterson.

Bloomfield; village in Bloomfield Township, Essex County, on Morris Canal, on Second River, and on New York and Greenwood Lake R. R., and Bloomfield Branch of Delaware, Lackawanna and Western R. R.................... Paterson.

Bloomingdale; village in south part of Pompton Township, Passaic County, on Pequonnock River, and on New York, Susquehanna and Western R. R............................ Greenwood Lake.

Bloomington; borough in northern part of Somerset County, on Raritan R. R., and on Delaware and Raritan Canal.... Somerville.

Bloombury; village in Bethlehem Township, Hunterdon County, on Musconetcong River, on New Jersey Central R. R., and Lehigh Valley R. R............................. Easton.

Blowenburg; village in Montgomery Township, Somerset County... Princeton.

Blue; brook in Union County, tributary to Green Brook .... Plainfield.

Blue Anchor; village in Winslow Township, Camden County Hammonton.

Blue Anchor Branch; brook in Winslow and Waterford townships, Camden County, tributary to Albertson Brook Hammonton.

Blue Bell; village in Franklin Township, Gloucester County Hammonton.

Bluefish Creek; passage in coast swamp in Middle Township, Cape May County...................................... Dennisville.

Boardville; village in Pompton Township, Passaic County, on Wanaque River, and on Ringwood Branch of New York and Greenwood Lake R. R .... Greenwood Lake.

Bog and Vly; meadows in southeastern part of Pequonnock Township, Morris County.................................. Morristown.

Bogota; village in Ridgefield Township, Bergen County, on Hackensack River, on the New York, Susquehanna and Western R. R., and the West Shore R. R.................. Paterson.

Boiling Springs; township in Bergen County; area, 4 square miles.. Paterson.

Bond; village in Eagleswood Township, Ocean County, on Atlantic coast .... Little Egg Harbor.

Bond; Life Saving Station, on Tucker Beach, Little Egg Harbor Township, Burlington County......................... Little Egg Harbor.

Bonhamtown; village in Raritan Township, Middlesex County, on Pennsylvania R. R.............................. Plainfield.

Boonton; township in Morris County; area, 7 square miles.. Morristown.

Boonton; city in Boonton and Hanover townships, Morris County, on Rockaway River, on Morris Canal, and on Boonton Branch of Delaware, Lackawanna and Western R. R.. Morristown.

Borden Mill Branch; brook in Plumstead and Jackson townships, Ocean County, flows into Ridgeway Branch...... Cassville.

Bordentown; village in Bordentown Township, Burlington County, on Delaware River, and at junction of Pennsylvania R. R. and Trenton Branch R. R., Amboy Division.. Bordentown.

22   A GEOGRAPHIC DICTIONARY OF NEW JERSEY.

Names of sheets.

Bordentown; township in Burlington County; area, 9 square
miles .... Bordentown.

Borton; landing in Willingboro Township, Burlington
County, on Rancocas Creek .... Burlington.

Boos Road; village in Delaware Township, Hunterdon
County, on Flemington Branch, Belvidere Division, Penn-
sylvania R. R. .... Lambertville.

Bottle Creek; passage in coast swamp in Dennis Township,
Cape May County .... Sea Isle.

Bound; creek rising in Clinton Township, Essex County,
forms boundary between Clinton Township and Newark
City and flows into Newark Bay .... Staten Island.

Bound; brook in Raritan and Piscataway Townships, Mid- { Somerville.
dlesex County, tributary to Green Brook.   { Plainfield.

Bound Brook; borough in Somerset County, at junction of
Green Brook with Raritan River, on Central R. R. of New
Jersey, and on Lehigh Valley R. R. .... Somerville.

Bowentown; village in Hopewell Township, Cumberland
County, on New Jersey Southern R. R. .... Bayside.

Bower; creek in Lawrence Township, Cumberland County,
flows into Cedar Creek .... Bridgeton.

Bowne; village in Delaware Township, Hunterdon County,
on Flemington Branch, Belvidere Division, Pennsylvania
R. R .... Lambertville.

Boyds Hotel; village in Manchester Township, Ocean
County .... Whitings.

Braddock; village in Winslow Township, Camden County .. Hammonton.

Braddock; island in north part of Great Egg Harbor, in
Upper Township, Cape May County .... Great Egg Harbor.

Braddock Mill; village in Medford Township, Burlington
County, on Kettle Run .... Mount Holly.

Bradevelt; village in Marlboro Township, Monmouth
County, on Freehold and New York R. R. .... Sandy Hook.

Bradway; station on New Jersey Southern R. R., in Pittsgrove Township, Salem County. .... Bridgeton.

Branch Mills; village in Westfield Township, Union County. Plainfield.

Branchburg; village in Eatontown Township, Monmouth
County .... Sandy Hook.

Branchburg; township in Somerset County; area, 20 square { High Bridge.
miles.   { Somerville.

Branchport; village in Eatontown Township, Monmouth
County, on New Jersey Southern R. R. and on Central
R. R. of New Jersey .... Sandy Hook.

Branchville; village in Frankford Township, Sussex County,
on Sussex R. R. .... Franklin.

Branchville Junction; village in Lafayette Township, at
junction of Sussex R. R. and New York, Susquehanna
and Western R. R., Sussex County .... Franklin.

Brass Castle; village in Washington Township, Warren
County .... Delaware Water Gap.

Bread and Cheese Run; brook in Shamong Township, Burlington County, flows into Friendship Creek .... Pemberton.

Breeches Branch; brook in Randolph Township, Burling- { Whitings.
ton County, flows into Oswego River.   { Little Egg Harbor.

Names of sheets.

Brick; township in Ocean County; area, 62 square miles... { Asbury Park. / Cassville.

Brick Church; village in East Orange Township, Essex County, on Morris and Essex Division, Delaware, Lackawanna and Western R. R .... Paterson.

Brick Yards; village in Manchester Township, Ocean County........... Whitings.

Bricksboro; village in Maurice River Township, Cumberland County, on West Jersey R. R........ Tuckahoe.

Bridge Sticks; creek in Fairfield Township, Cumberland { Bridgeton. / County, flows into Ogden Creek. { Bayside.

Bridgeboro; village in Delran Township, Burlington County. Burlington.

Bridgepoint; village in Montgomery Township, Somerset County, on No Pike Brook .... Princeton.

Bridgeport; village in Bass River Township, Burlington County, on Ives Branch of Wading River ...... Little Egg Harbor.

Bridgeport; village in Logan Township, Gloucester County, on Raccoon Creek .... Chester.

Bridgeton; township in Cumberland County; area, 13 square miles........ Bridgeton.

Bridgeton; city in Bridgeton Township, Cumberland County. Bridgeton.

Bridgeton Junction; village in Bridgeton Township, Cumberland County........ Bridgeton.

Bridgeville; village in Oxford Township, Warren County, on Pequest River and on Lehigh and Hudson River R. R.... Delaware Water Gap.

Bridgewater; township in Somerset County; area, 44 square miles........ Somerville.

Brielle; village in Wall Township, Monmouth County, on Philadelphia and Long Branch R. R........ Asbury Park.

Brigantine; village on coast of Galloway Township, Atlantic County........ Atlantic City.

Brigantine; inlet projecting from Atlantic Ocean into Galloway Township, Atlantic County........ Atlantic City.

Brigantine; channel in coast swamp in Galloway Township, Atlantic County, flows into Brigantine Inlet........ Atlantic City.

Brigantine; beach on coast of Galloway Township, Atlantic County........ Atlantic City.

Brigantine; life-saving station on Brigantine Beach........ Atlantic City.

Brighton; village in Andover Township, Sussex County, on Lehigh and Hudson River R. R........ Hackettstown.

Brindletown; village in Plumstead Township, Ocean County, on South Run........ Bordentown.

Broad Creek Thorofare; passage in coast swamp in Galloway Township, Atlantic County .... Atlantic City.

Broad Lane; village in Monroe Township, Gloucester County Hammonton.

Broad Thorofare; passage in coast swamp in Egg Harbor Township, Atlantic County, connecting Scull Bay with Great Egg Harbor........ Great Egg Harbor.

Broadway; village in northern part of Franklin Township, Warren County .... Easton.

Brockaway; brook in Mullica Township, Atlantic County, flows into Mullica River........ Mullica.

Brook Valley; village in southern part of Pequonnock Township, Morris County, on Stony Brook........ Morristown.

Names of sheets.

Brookdale; village in northern part of Bloomfield Township, Essex County, on Morris Canal.......................... Paterson.

Brooklyn; village in Byram Township, Sussex County, at outlet of Lake Hopatcong.............................. Lake Hopatcong.

Brookside; village in northeast part of Mendham Township, Morris County... Lake Hopatcong.

Brookville; village in southern part of Delaware Township, Hunterdon County, on Delaware River and on Belvidere Division, Pennsylvania R. R.............................. Lambertville.

Brotzmanville; village in Pahaquarry Township, Warren County, on Delaware River............................... Bushkill Falls.

Brown; village in northern part of West Milford Township, Passaic County, on southern coast of Greenwood Lake.. Greenwood Lake.

Brown; village in Lumberton Township, Burlington County, on Philadelphia, Marlton and Medford R. R.............. Mount Holly.

Browns Mills; village in Pemberton Township, Burlington County, on Rancocas Creek............................... Pemberton.

Browns Mills; station in Pembroke Township, Burlington County, on Philadelphia and Long Branch R. R......... Pemberton.

Browning; village in Knowlton Township, Warren County, on Delaware River and on Delaware, Lackawanna and Western R. R.. Delaware Water Gap.

Browntown; village in Madison Township, Middlesex County.. New Brunswick.

Brownsville; village in Gloucester Township, Camden County, on North Branch of Timber Creek .... Philadelphia.

Buck; island in swamp in Independence Township, Warren County.. Hackettstown.

Buck; creek in Washington and Hamilton Townships, Mercer County, flows into Crosswick Creek...................... Bordentown.

Buck Bar; island off western coast of Wallpack Township. Sussex County, in Delaware River .... Wallpack.

Buckabear; pond in West Milford Township, Passaic County. Greenwood Lake.

Buckhorn; creek rising in Oxford Township, flows southwest into Delaware River in northwest part of Harmony Township, Warren County...................................... Delaware Water Gap.

Buckingham; village in Manchester Township, Ocean County, on Philadelphia and Long Branch R. R.................. Whitings.

Buckmire; pond in southeast part of Green Township, Sussex County.. Hackettstown.

Buckshutem; swamp in Millville, Commercial, and Downe Townships, Cumberland County .... Bridgeton.

Buckshutem; village in Commercial Township, Cumberland County.. Bridgeton.

Budd; lake in central part of Mount Olive Township, Morris { Hackettstown. County. { Lake Hopatcong.

Buddstown; village in Southampton Township, Burlington County.. Pemberton.

Buena Vista; village in Greenwich Township, Cumberland County.. Bayside.

Buena Vista; village on West Jersey R. R., in Atlantic County.. Hammonton.

Buena Vista; township in Atlantic County; area, 58 square miles.. Hammonton.

Names of sheets.

Buffin; brook in Pemberton Township, Burlington County, tributary to Pole Bridge Brook .... Pemberton.

Bull; creek in Washington Township, Burlington County, flows into Mullica River .... Mullica.

Bull; island off coast of Kingwood and Delaware townships, Hunterdon County, in Delaware River .... Doylestown.

Bull Branch; brook in Randolph Township, Burlington County, flows into west branch of Wading River .... Mullica.

Bull Ferry; village in North Bergen Township, Hudson County, on Hudson River .... Harlem.

Bulltown; village in Washington Township, Burlington County .... Mullica.

Burkville; village in Millstone Township, Monmouth County. Cassville.

Burleigh; village in Middle Township, Cape May County, on Anglesea R. R. .... Dennisville.

Burlington; county in southern part of State; area, 899 square miles.

Germantown.
Hammonton.
Philadelphia.
Burlington.
Mount Holly.
Bordentown.
Pemberton.
Mullica.
Whitings.
Little Egg Harbor.
Atlantic City.

Burlington; township in Burlington County; area, 19 square miles .... Burlington.

Burlington; island in Delaware River, in Burlington Township, Burlington County .... Burlington.

Burlington; city in Burlington Township, Burlington County, on Delaware River and on Amboy Division, Pennsylvania R. R. .... Burlington.

Burnt Bridge Branch; brook in Woodland Township, Burlington County; flows into Burrs Mill Brook .... Pemberton.

Burnt Mill; village in Branchburg Township, Somerset County, at junction of Lamington River and North Branch of Raritan River .... Somerville.

Burnett; brook, tributary to North Branch of Raritan River, rises in Randolph Township, and forms boundary between Mendham and Chester Townships, Morris County .... Lake Hopatcong.

Burrough Hole; passage in coast swamp, in Upper Township, Cape May County .... Sea Isle.

Burrs Mill; brook in Woodland and Southampton Townships, Burlington County; flows into Friendship Creek .. Pemberton.

Burrs Mill; village in Southampton Township, Burlington County, on Burrs Mill Brook .... Pemberton.

Burrsville; village in Brick Township, Ocean County, on Metedconk River .... Asbury Park.

Burt Creek; village in Sayreville Township, Middlesex County .... New Brunswick.

Bustleton; village in Florence Township, Burlington County. Burlington.

Butler Place; village in Woodland Township, Burlington County .... Pemberton.

Names of sheets.

Buttonwood Corners; village in East Amwell Township, Hunterdon County.. Lambertville.

Butzville; village in Oxford Township, Warren County, on Pequest River, on Delaware, Lackawanna and Western R. R., and on Lehigh and Hudson River R. R .... Delaware Water Gap.

Byram; township in Sussex County; area, 36 square miles.. { Hackettstown. Lake Hopatcong. Franklin.

Byram; cove, an arm of Lake Hopatcong indenting eastern coast of Byram Township, Sussex County .... Lake Hopatcong.

Byram; village in Kingwood Township, Hunterdon County, on Delaware River and on Belvidere Division, Pennsylvania R. R.. Doylestown.

Cabin Branch; brook in Jackson and Manchester townships, Ocean County, flows into Ridgway Branch......... Cassville.

Cakepoulin; creek in Franklin Township, Hunterdon County, tributary to South Branch of Raritan River............. High Bridge.

Calais; village in Randolph Township, Morris County...... Lake Hopatcong.

Caldwell; village in Caldwell Township, Essex County..... Morristown.

Caldwell; township in Essex County; area, 28 square miles. { Paterson. Morristown.

Caldwell Junction; village in Caldwell Township, Essex County .... Paterson.

Calico; village in Bass River Township, Burlington County. Little Egg Harbor.

Califon; village in Tewksbury Township, Hunterdon County, on South Branch of Raritan River, and on High Bridge Branch of New Jersey Central R. R........................ High Bridge.

Cambridge; village in Delran Township, Burlington County, on Amboy Division, Pennsylvania R. R.................... Burlington.

Camden; county in southwestern part of the State; area, 226 square miles. { Philadelphia. Glassboro. Mount Holly. Hammonton. Mullica.

Camden; city in Camden County, on Delaware River .... Philadelphia.

Camp Gaw; village in central part of Franklin Township, Bergen County, on New York, Susquehanna and Western R. R... Ramapo.

Camp Meeting; lake between Asbury Park and Ocean Grove, Neptune Township, Monmouth County .... Asbury Park.

Canistear; village in Vernon Township, Sussex County..... Greenwood Lake.

Canoe; brook in Livingston and Milburn townships, Essex County, tributary to Passaic River. { Morristown. Plainfield.

Canton; village in Lower Alloways Township, Salem County, Bayside.

Cape Island; sound in Lower Township, Cape May County.. Cape May.

Cape Island; creek in Lower Township, Cape May County.. Cape May.

Cape May; county, in extreme southern part of the State; area, 442 square miles. { Cape May. Dennisville. Tuckahoe. Great Egg Harbor. Sea Isle.

Cape May; city in southern part of Cape May County, on Cape May and Sewell Point R. R .... Cape May.

Names of sheets.

Cape May; life-saving station at southwestern extremity of Lower Township, Cape May County .... Cape May.

Cape May; light-house at southwest extremity of Lower Township, Cape May County .... Cape May.

Cape May and Sewell Point; railroad running west along southern shore of Lower Township, Cape May County, connects with West Jersey R. R. .... Cape May.

Cape May Court-House; town in Cape May County, on West Jersey R. R. .... Dennisville.

Cape May Point; borough in Cape May County .... Cape May.

Carasaljo; lake, an enlargement of Metedeconk River, in Brick Township, Ocean County .... Asbury Park.

Cary; village in Roxbury Township, Morris County, on Drakers Brook and on High Bridge Branch of Central R. R. of New Jersey .... Lake Hopatcong.

Carlisle Run; brook in Alloways Township, Salem County, flows into Alloways Creek .... Salem.

Carlsburg; village in Deerfield Township, Cumberland County .... Bridgeton.

Carlstadt; town in western part of Lodi Township, Bergen County, on New Jersey and New York R. R. .... Paterson.

Carmantown; village in Hamilton Township, Atlantic County. { Mullica. { Great Egg Harbor.

Carmel; village in Bridgeton Township, Cumberland County. Bridgeton.

Carpentersville; village in Pohatcong Township, Warren County, on Delaware River and on Pennsylvania R. R., Belvidere Division .... Easton.

Carrs Tavern; village in Millstone Township, Monmouth County .... Cassville.

Carter; brook in South Brunswick Township, Middlesex County, tributary to Millstone River .... Princeton.

Carteret; village in Woodbridge Township, Middlesex County, on New York and Long Branch R. R. .... Staten Island.

Carvel; island in Manahawken Bay, in Stafford Township, Ocean County .... Long Beach.

Cassville; village in Jackson Township, Ocean County ...... Cassville.

Castle; point of land off eastern coast of Hoboken City, projecting into Hudson River .... Staten Island.

Catawba; village in Hamilton Township, Atlantic County .. Great Egg Harbor.

Catfish; pond in Stillwater Township, Sussex County .... Wallpack.

Cavan; point of land projecting from southern coast of Jersey City into New York Upper Bay .... Staten Island.

Cave Cabin Branch; brook in Ocean and Lacey townships, Ocean County, flows into North Branch of Forked River. Whitings.

Cecil; village in Monroe Township, Gloucester County, on Hospitality Branch of Great Egg Harbor .... Hammonton.

Cedar; brook rising in Fanwood Township, flows through Plainfield Township, Union County, and empties into Bound Brook, Piscataway Township, Middlesex County Plainfield.

Cedar; brook rising in Hamilton Township, flows through portion of Weymouth Township, Atlantic County, into South River. { Tuckahoe. { Great Egg Harbor.

Cedar; brook in Alloways Township, Salem County, flows into Alloways Creek .... Salem.

Names of sheets.

Cedar; brook in Monroe Township, Middlesex County, flows into Cranbury Brook .... New Brunswick.

Cedar; creek in Lower Township, Cape May County .... Cape May.

Cedar; creek on boundary between Berkeley and Lacey townships, Ocean County, flows into Barnegat Bay. { Whitings. Barnegat.

Cedar; creek in Downe Township, Cumberland County, flows into Dividing Creek .... Bridgeton.

Cedar; creek in Lawrence Township, Cumberland County, flows into Delaware River. { Bridgeton. Bayside.

Cedar; lake in Blairstown Township, Warren County .... Hackettstown.

Cedar; pond in West Milford Township, Passaic County .... Greenwood Lake.

Cedar Bonnet; group of Islands in Manahawken Bay, in Stafford Township, Ocean County .... Long Beach.

Cedar Branch; brook in Hammonton Township, Atlantic County, flows into Great Swamp Branch of Mullica River. { Hammonton. Mullica.

Cedar Branch; brook in Weymouth Township, Atlantic County, flows into Great Egg Harbor River .... Great Egg Harbor.

Cedar Branch; brook in Landis Township, Cumberland County, tributary to Manantico Creek .... Tuckahoe.

Cedar Branch; brook in Maurice River Township, Cumberland County, flows into Manumuskin River .... Tuckahoe.

Cedar Bridge; village in Union Township, Ocean County... Whitings.

Cedar Bridge; brook in Brick Township, Ocean County, flows into Metedeconk River .... Asbury Park.

Cedar Bridge; village in Brick Township, Ocean County, at mouth of Cedar Bridge Brook............................. Asbury Park.

Cedar Brook; village in Winslow Township, Camden County, on Philadelphia and Reading R. R......................... Hammonton.

Cedar Creek; village in Lacey Township, Ocean County ... Barnegat.

Cedar Creek; life-saving station on Island Beach in Lacey Township, Ocean County .... Barnegat.

Cedar Grove; village in Princeton Township, Mercer County Princeton.

Cedar Grove; village in Dover Township, Ocean County .... Barnegat.

Cedar Grove; village in Caldwell Township, Essex County, on Peckman Brook.. Paterson.

Cedar Grove; village in Stafford Township, Ocean County.. Little Egg Harbor.

Cedar Grove; village in Dennis Township, Cape May County. Dennisville.

Cedar Lake; village in Buena Vista Township, Atlantic County, on New Jersey Southern R. R..................... Hammonton.

Cedar Run; brook in Southampton Township, Burlington County, flows into Rancocas Creek......................... Pemberton.

Cedar Run; brook in Stafford and Eagleswood townships, Ocean County, flows into Little Egg Harbor. { Little Egg Harbor. Long Beach.

Cedar Run; village in Stafford Township, Ocean County, on Cedar Run... Little Egg Harbor.

Cedar Swamp; creek rising in Dennis Township, flows northeast through Upper Township, Cape May County, into Tuckahoe River. { Dennisville. Sea Isle. Great Egg Harbor.

Cedarville; village in Lawrence Township, Cumberland County, on Cedar Creek................................... Bridgeton.

Center; township in Camden County; area, 13 square miles.. Philadelphia.

Center Grove; village in Lawrence Township, Cumberland County.. Bridgeton.

Center Square; village in Logan Township, Gloucester County .... Chester.

Names of sheets.

Center Square; station on Delaware River R. R., in Logan Township, Gloucester County .... Chester.

Centerton; village in Pittsgrove Township, Salem County .. Glassboro.

Centerton; village in Mount Laurel Township, Burlington County .... Mount Holly.

Centerville; village in Shrewsbury Township, Monmouth County .... Sandy Hook.

Centerville; village in central part of Galloway Township, Atlantic County .... Atlantic City.

Centerville; village in Readington Township, Hunterdon County, on Pleasant Run. { High Bridge. Somerville.

Centerville; part of Bayonne City on New York Upper Bay and on Central R. R. of New Jersey .... Staten Island.

Chadwick; village on reef in Dover Township, Ocean County, on Philadelphia and Long Branch R. R .... Barnegat.

Chadwick; life-saving station on reef in Dover Township, Ocean County .... Barnegat.

Chairville; village in Medford Township, Burlington County, at junction of Bear Swamp River and Little Creek ...... Mount Holly.

Chamberlain; brook in Lacey Township, Ocean County, tributary to Cedar Creek. { Whitings. Barnegat.

Chambers; brook heading in Readington Township, Hunterdon County, flows into North Branch of Raritan River in Branchburg Township, Somerset County. } High Bridge. Somerville.

Chambersburg; borough, part of Trenton, in Mercer County .. Bordentown.

Changewater; village in Washington Township, Warren County, on Musconetcong River and on Delaware, Lackawanna and Western R. R .... High Bridge.

hannel; creek in Eagleswood Township, Ocean County, flows into Little Egg Harbor .... Little Egg Harbor.

Chapel Hill; light on Chapel Hill in Middletown Township, Monmouth County .... Sandy Hook.

Chapel Hill; village in Middletown Township, Monmouth County .... Sandy Hook.

Charleston; village in Willingboro Township, Burlington County .... Burlington.

Charleston Springs; village in Millstone Township, Monmouth County .... Cassville.

Charlestown; village in Bethlehem Township, Hunterdon County .... High Bridge.

Charlottesburg; village in West Milford Township, Passaic County, on Pequonnock River and on New York, Susquehanna and Western R. R .... Greenwood Lake.

Chatham; township in Morris County; area, 23 square miles . { Morristown. Plainfield.

Chatham; village in Chatham Township, Morris County, on Passaic River, and on Delaware, Lackawanna and Western R. R .... Plainfield.

Chatsworth; village in Woodland Township, Burlington County .... Pemberton.

Cheapside; village in Livingston Township, Essex County . Morristown.

Cheesequake; creek forming partial boundary between Sayreville and Madison townships, Middlesex County, flows into Raritan Bay .... New Brunswick.

Names of sheets.

Cherry Hill; village in Midland Township, Bergen County, on Hackensack River and on New Jersey and New York R. R. .... Paterson.

Cherry Ridge; village in Vernon Township, Sussex County. Greenwood Lake.

Cherryville; village in Franklin Township, Hunterdon County .... High Bridge.

Chesilhurst; village in Waterford Township, Camden County, on Camden and Atlantic R. R. .... Hammonton.

Chester; township in Morris County; area, 30 square miles. { Somerville. Lake Hopatcong.

Chester; township in Burlington County; area, 19 square miles. { Mount Holly. Burlington.

Chester; town in Chester Township, Morris County, on Chester Branch of Delaware, Lackawanna and Western R. R... Lake Hopatcong.

Chester; island in Delaware River forming part of Greenwich and Logan townships, Gloucester County................. Chester.

Chesterfield; township in Burlington County; area, 22 square miles .... Bordentown.

Chesterville; village in Delran Township, Burlington County, on Swede Run.. Burlington.

Chestnut; branch of Mantua Creek, rises in Glassboro Township flows north through Mantua Township, Gloucester County. { Philadelphia. Glassboro.

Chestnut Creek; peninsula projecting from Galloway Township, Atlantic County, into the coast swamp............. Little Egg Harbor.

Chestnut Ridge; village in Orvil Township, Bergen County. Ramapo.

Chestnut Run; brook in Stow Creek Township, Cumberland County, tributary to Newport Creek...................... Bayside.

Chews Landing; village in Gloucester Township, Camden County, on North branch of Timber Creek................ Philadelphia.

Chicken Bone; hill in Ocean Township, Ocean County; elevation, 104 feet.. Whitings.

Chimney Rock; mountain in Bridgewater Township, Somerset County; altitude, 418 feet.............................. Somerville.

Chincapin Branch; brook in Maurice River Township, Cumberland County, flows west into Manumuskin River..... Tuckahoe.

Chingarora; creek in Raritan Township, Monmouth County, flows into Raritan Bay.................................. Sandy Hook.

Church; landing on coast of Lower Penns Neck Township, Salem County.. Wilmington.

Cinnaminson; township in Burlington County; area, 12 square miles. { Burlington. Mount Holly. Philadelphia. Germantown.

Cinnaminson; village in Cinnaminson Township, Burlington County .... Burlington.

City Line Station; village in Haddon Township, Camden County, on Camden and Atlantic R. R..................... Philadelphia.

Clam; island in Barnegat Bay, in Ocean Township, Ocean County... Barnegat.

Clam; creek in Berkeley Township, Ocean County, flows into Barnegat Bay.. Barnegat.

Claremont; part of Jersey City on Central R. R. of New Jersey and on New York Upper Bay..................... Staten Island.

Names of sheets.

Clark; township in Union County; area, 5 square miles...... Plainfield.

Clark; village in Millville Township, Cumberland County.. Bridgeton.

Clark; landing in Galloway Township, Atlantic County, on
Mullica River... Mullica.

Clark Branch; brook in Hopewell Township, Cumberland
County, flows into Cohansey Creek........................ Salem.

Clark Branch; brook in Winslow and Waterford Town- ⎫ Hammonton.
ships, Camden County, flows into Mechesactauxin ⎬
branch of Mullicas River. ⎭ Mullica.

Clarksboro; village in East Greenwich Township, Gloucester
County, on West Jersey R. R............................... Philadelphia.

Clarksburg; village in Millstone Township, Monmouth
County... Cassville.

Clarkstown; village in Hamilton Township, Atlantic County. Great Egg Harbor.

Clarksville; village in West Windsor Township, Mercer
County... Princeton.

Clarksville; village in Lebanon Township, Hunterdon County,
on Spruce Run and on Delaware, Lackawanna and West-
ern R. R. .... High Bridge.

Clay Pit; creek in Middletown Township, Monmouth County,
flows into Navesink River................................. Sandy Hook.

Clayton; township in Gloucester County; area, 22 square
miles.. Glassboro.

Clayton; borough in Gloucester County, on West Jersey R. R. Glassboro.

Clayton Corner; village in Manalapan Township, Monmouth
County... Cassville.

Clear Run; brook in Maurice River Township, Cumberland
County, tributary to Muskee Creek .... Tuckahoe.

Clear Run; brook in Maurice River Township, Cumberland
County, flows into Maurice River......................... Tuckahoe.

Clementon; village in Gloucester Township, Camden County,
on Philadelphia and Atlantic City R. R................... Mount Holly.

Clements; village in Greenwich Township, Gloucester County,
on Delaware River R. R.................................... Chester.

Cliffwood; village in Matawan Township, Monmouth County. Sandy Hook.

Clifton; town in Acquackanonck Township, Passaic County,
on New York, Lake Erie and Western R. R., and on Boonton
branch of Delaware, Lackawanna and Western R. R..... Paterson.

Clinton; township in Hunterdon County; area, 28 square
miles.. High Bridge.

Clinton; township in Essex County; area, 7 square miles... ⎰ Plainfield.
⎱ Staten Island.

Clinton; town in Clinton Township, Hunterdon County, on
South branch of Raritan River and on Clinton branch of
Lehigh Valley R. R. .... High Bridge.

Clinton; village in Caldwell Township, Essex County........ Morristown.

Clinton; village in West Milford Township, Passaic County. Greenwood Lake.

Clonmell; creek in Greenwich Township, Gloucester County,
flows into Delaware River................................. Chester.

Closter; village in Harrington Township, Bergen County, on
Tienekill Creek and on Northern R. R. of New Jersey.   Harlem.

Clove; river in Wantage Township, Sussex County, enters ⎰ Port Jervis.
the Papakating Creek at Deckertown. ⎱ Franklin.

Clover Hill; village in Hillsboro Township, Somerset County. Lambertville.

Names of sheets.

Clyde; village in Franklin Township, Somerset County, on Millstone branch of Pennsylvania R. R .... Princeton.

Coate; point on coast of Dover Township, Ocean County... Barnegat.

Cobbs Island; village in Lower Penns Neck Township, Salem County .... Salem.

Cohansey; village in Hopewell Township, Cumberland County .... Salem.

Cohansey; light-house on coast of Greenwich Township, Cumberland County .... Bayside.

Cohansey; creek rising in Alloway Township, Salem County, ⎰ Salem.
flows southerly through Cumberland County into Dela- ⎱ Bridgeton.
ware River. ⎰ Bayside.

Cokesburg; village in Tewksbury Township, Hunterdon County .... High Bridge.

Cold Spring; village in Lower Township, Cape May County, on West Jersey R. R .... Cape May.

Cold Spring; life-saving station on southern shore of Lower Township, Cape May County.......................... .... Cape May.

Cold Spring; inlet projecting from Atlantic Ocean into southeast shore of Lower Township, Cape May County .... Cape May.

Colemantown; village in Mount Laurel Township, Burlington County... Mount Holly.

Coleville; village in Montage Township, Sussex County, on Clove River... Port Jervis.

Collier Mills; village in Plumstead Township, Ocean County Cassville.

Collingswood; borough in Haddon Township, Camden County, on Camden and Atlantic R. R .... Philadelphia.

Colts Neck; village in Atlantic Township, Monmouth County, on Yellow Brook................................. Sandy Hook.

Columbia; village in Knowlton Township, Warren County, on Delaware River and on New York, Susquehanna and Western R. R.. Delaware Water Gap

Columbia Bridge; village in Chatham Township, Morris County, on Passaic River................................... Morristown.

Columbus; village in Mansfield Township, Burlington County, on Kinkora branch, Amboy division, Pennsylvania R. R... Bordentown.

Calwell; village in Mullica Township, Camden County...... Hammonton.

Comfort; point extending from Raritan Township, Monmouth County, into Raritan Bay................................ Sandy Hook.

Comical Corner; village in Pemberton Township, Burlington County.. Pemberton.

Commercial; township in Cumberland County; area, 35 ⎰ Tuckahoe.
square miles. ⎱ Maurice Cove.
⎰ Bridgeton.

Communipaw; part of Jersey City on New York Upper Bay. Staten Island.

Como; lake in Wall Township, Monmouth County .... Asbury Park.

Compton; creek in Middletown Township, Monmouth County, flows into Sandy Hook Bay................................. Sandy Hook.

Conaskonk; point extending from Raritan Township, Monmouth County, into Raritan Bay .... Sandy Hook.

Conklin; island in Union Township, Ocean County, in Barnegat Bay... Long Beach.

Connecticut Farms; village in Union Township, Union County .... Plainfield.

Names of sheets.

Conover; beacon on coast of Middletown Township, Monmouth County .... Sandy Hook.

Conoverville; village on boundary between Galloway and Egg Harbor townships, Atlantic County .... Atlantic City.

Constable; point of land projecting from east coast of Bayonne City, Hudson County, into New York Upper Bay .... Staten Island.

Convent; village in Morris Township, Morris County, on Delaware, Lackawanna and Western R. R .... Morristown.

Cook; pond in Blairstown Township, Warren County .... Hackettstown.

Cook; pond in Brick Township, Ocean County .... Asbury Park.

Cooks Bridge; Village in Hanover Township, Morris County, on Passaic River.. Morristown.

Cookstown; village in New Hanover Township, Burlington County, on North Run .... Bordentown.

Cool Run; brook in Alloway Township, Salem County, flows into Alloways Creek .... Salem.

Coontown; village in Warren Township, Somerset County.. Somerville.

Cooper; village in West Milford Township, Passaic County, on Greenwood Lake at head of Wanaque River and on New York and Greenwood Lake R. R .... Greenwood Lake.

Cooper; station in Logan Township, Gloucester County, on Delaware River R. R .... Chester.

Cooper; point of land projecting from Camden City into Delaware River .... Philadelphia.

Cooper; creek rising in Waterford Township, flows through { Philadelphia. Camden County, into Delaware River at Camden City. { Mount Holly.

Cooper Branch; brook in Woodland Township, Burlington County, tributary to Mount Misery Brook................ Pemberton.

Cooper Branch; brook in Waterford Township, Camden County, flows into Mechesactauxin Branch of Mullica River .... Hammonton.

Coopers Creek, North Branch of; creek rising in Waterford } Philadelphia. Township, Camden County, flows through Delaware } Mount Holly. Township, tributary to Coopers Creek. }

Cooperstown; village in Delaware Township, Camden County, on Coopers Creek.................................. Philadelphia.

Cooperstown; village in Willingboro Township, Burlington County.. Burlington.

Copper; creek in Kingwood Township, Hunterdon County, tributary to Delaware River............................... Easton.

Copper Hill; village in Raritan Township, Hunterdon County, on Flemington Branch Belvidere Division R. R., and on Neshanic River .... Lambertville.

Copperas; mountain range extending along western { Greenwood Lake. boundary of Rockaway Township, Morris County. { Morristown. { Lake Hopatcong.

Cordery; creek in Galloway Township, Atlantic County, flows into Reed Bay .... Atlantic City.

Cordery Thorofare; passage in coast swamp in Galloway Township, Atlantic County .... Atlantic City

Cornell Run; brook in Deerfield Township, Cumberland County, flows into Cohansey Creek...................... Bridgeton,

Corona; village in Lodi Township, Bergen County, on New Jersey and New York R. R................................. Paterson.

Bull. 118——3

34   A GEOGRAPHIC DICTIONARY OF NEW JERSEY.

Names of sheets.

Corson; inlet projecting from Atlantic Ocean into coast of
Upper Township, Cape May County .... Sea Isle.

Corson; sound in coast swamp in Upper Township, Cape
May County... Sea Isle.

Corson Inlet; life-saving station on coast of Upper Township, Cape May County................................ Sea Isle.

Cossa Boone Branch; brook in Landis Township, Cumberland County, flows into Bears Head Branch .... Tuckahoe.

Cotterall; brook in Brick Township, Ocean County, flows
into Metedeconk River................................ Asbury Park.

Course; landing in Mannington Township, Salem County,
on Salem Creek....................................... Salem.

Cow Tongue; point of land projecting from eastern coast of
Byram Township, Sussex County, into Lake Hopatcong. Lake Hopatcong.

Cow Yard; brook rising in South Brunswick Township,
and forming boundary between North and South Brunswick townships, Middlesex County, and tributary to
Lawrence Brook. { Princeton. New Brunswick. }

Cox; village in Eagleswood Township, Ocean County, on
Tuckahoe R. R., ... Little Egg Harbor.

Coxall; creek in Lower Township, Cape May County .... Cape May.

Cranberry; hill in Atlantic Township, Monmouth County;
elevation, 244 feet.................................... Sandy Hook.

Cranberry; brook in Manchester Township, Ocean County,
and Pemberton Township, Burlington County, tributary
to Pole Bridge Brook. { Whitings. Pemberton. }

Cranberry Hall; village in New Hanover Township, Burlington County .... Bordentown.

Cranberry Park; village in New Hanover Township, Burlington County .... Bordentown.

Cranbury; township in Middlesex County; area, 18 square
miles. { Princeton. New Brunswick. }

Cranbury; village in Cranbury Township, Middlesex County,
on Cranbury Brook .... Princeton.

Cranbury; station on Camden and Amboy division Pennsylvania R. R., in Cranbury Township, Middlesex County New Brunswick.

Cranbury; brook in Monroe and Cranbury Townships, Middlesex County, flows into Millstone River. { New Brunswick. Princeton. }

Cranetown; village in Randolph Township, Morris County. Lake Hopatcong.

Cranford; township in Union County; area, 6 square miles.. Plainfield.

Cranford; village in Cranford Township, Union County, on
Rahway River and on Central R. R. of New Jersey..... Plainfield.

Cranford; hill in Middleton Township, Monmouth County;
elevation, 391 feet.................................... Sandy Hook.

Crawford Corner; village in Middleton Township, Monmouth County .... Sandy Hook.

Cream Ridge; village in Upper Freehold Township, Monmouth County, on Pemberton and Hightstown R. R..... Bordentown.

Creesville; village in Washington Township, Gloucester
County.. Philadelphia.

Cresse Throrofare; passage in coast swamp in Middle Township, Cape May County .... Dennisville.

Cresskill; town in Palisade Township, Bergen County, on
Northern R. R. of New Jersey and on Tienekill Creek... Harlem.

Names of sheets.

Crook Horn; passage in coast swamp in Upper Township, Cape May County... Sea Isle.

Crooked; creek in Middle Township, Cape May County, flowing into Nicholas Channel .... Dennisville.

Crooked Throrofare; passage in coast swamp in Middle Township, Cape May County............................... Dennisville.

Cropwell; village in Evesham Township, Burlington County, on Philadelphia, Marlton and Medford R. R .... Mount Holly.

Cross; creek in Lawrence Township, Cumberland County, flows into Back Creek .... Bayside.

Cross Ditch; passage in coast swamp in Fairfield Township, Cumberland County .....'............................... Bayside.

Cross Keys; village in Monroe Township, Gloucester County. Glassboro

Cross Roads; village in Medford Township, Burlington County .... Mount Holly.

Crosswick; creek heading in two streams, the North Run ⎫
and the South Run, flows across Ocean County and on ⎬ Cassville.
boundary between Burlington and Mercer counties into ⎰ Bordentown.
Delaware River. ⎭

Crosswick; village in Chesterfield Township, Burlington County, on Crosswick Creek .... Bordentown.

Crow; creek rising in Middle Township, Cape May County, flows into Dennis Creek...................................... Dennisville.

Crowder Branch; brook in Maurice River Township, Cumberland County, flowing into Maurice River.............. Tuckahoe.

Crowfoot; village in Evesham Township, Burlington County. Mount Holly.

Crowleytown; village in Washington Township, Burlington County .... Mullica.

Croton; village in Delaware and Raritan townships, Hunterdon County, on Wickecheoke Creek .... High Bridge.

Croyden; village in Bristol Township, Bucks County .... Burlington.

Cruser; brook in Montgomery Township, Somerset County, tributary to No Pike Brook .... Princeton.

Crystal Lake; village in Franklin Township, Bergen County, on New York, Susquehanna and Western R. R............. Ramapo.

Cuckolds; brook in Bridgewater Township, Somerset County, tributary to Raritan River .... Somerville.

Cullier Run; brook in Mannington Township, Salem County, flows into Mannington Creek............................... Salem.

Culvert; pond in Franklin Township, Sussex County......... Wallpack.

Culver; gap in eastern part of Sandyston Township, Sussex County .... Wallpack.

Cumberland; county in southwest part of the State; area, 685 square miles.
⎧ Bayside.
⎪ Salem.
⎪ Glassboro.
⎬ Bridgeton.
⎪ Maurice Cove.
⎪ Dennisville.
⎪ Tuckahoe.
⎩ Hammonton.

Cumberland; village in Maurice River Township, Cumberland County, on Manumuskin River....................... Tuckahoe.

Cushetunk; mountain in eastern part of Clinton Township, Hunterdon County; greatest elevation is 839 feet .... High Bridge.

Names of sheets.

Cuthbert Station; village in Haddon Township, Camden County, on Camden and Atlantic R. R. .... Philadelphia.

Dacosta; village in Hammonton Township, Atlantic County, on Camden and Atlantic R. R. .... Hammonton.

Dalbows; landing on coast of Oldmans Township, Salem County .... Chester.

Daniel; island in Little Egg Harbor, Eagleswood Township, Ocean County .... Long Beach.

Danville; village in Hope Township, extending across boundary into Independence Township, Warren County, on Lehigh and Hudson River R. R. .... Hackettstown.

Daretown; village in Upper Pittsgrove Township, Salem County .... Salem.

Darlington; village in Hohokus Township, Bergen County, on Ramapo River .... Ramapo.

Davidstown; village in Gloucester Township, Camden County .... Philadelphia.

Davis; village in Upper Freehold Township, Monmouth County, on Pemberton and Hightstown R. R. .... Bordentown.

Davis; cove indenting eastern coast of Byram Township, Sussex County... Lake Hopatcong.

Dayton; village in South Brunswick Township, Middlesex County. .... Princeton.

Dayton; creek in Lawrence Township, Cumberland County flows into Back Creek.................................... Bayside.

De Hansey; brook in Greenwich Township, Gloucester County, tributary to Still Run .... Chester.

De Kays; village in Vernon Township, Sussex County, on Lehigh and Hudson River R. R. .... Greenwood Lake.

Deacon; village in Burlington Township, Burlington County, on Burlington Branch, Amboy Division, Pennsylvania R. R. .... Burlington.

Dead; river in Bernard Township, Somerset County, tributary to Passaic River.................................... Somerville.

Dead; creek in Newark, Essex County, tributary to Maple Island Creek... Staten Island.

Dead Thorofare; passage in coast swamp in Middle Township, Cape May County.................................... Dennisville.

Deak Tree; run in Montgomery Township, Somerest County, tributary to No Pike Brook...................... Princeton.

Deal; lake in Ocean Township, Monmouth County, flows into Atlantic Ocean.. Asbury Park.

Deal; village in Ocean Township, Monmouth County........ Sandy Hook.

Deal; coast village in Ocean Township, Monmouth County, Asbury Park.

Deal Beach; village in Ocean Township, Monmouth County, on New York and Long Branch R. R. .... Asbury Park.

Deans; village in South Brunswick Township, Middlesex County, on Pennsylvania R. R. .... Princeton.

Deb Thorofare; passage in coast swamp in Calloway Township, Atlantic County....................................... Atlantic City.

Decker; pond in Vernon Township, Sussex County.......... Franklin.

Deckertown; town in Wantage Township, Sussex County, on New York, Susquehanna and Western R. R. .... Franklin.

Deep; creek in Lower Alloways Creek Township, Salem County, flows into Delaware River................... Bayside.

Names of sheets.

Deep; point projecting from Little Egg Harbor townships, Burlington County, into Great Bay .... Little Egg Harbor

Deep Run; brook in Shamony Township, Burlington County, flows into Batsto River. { Pemberton. Mullica. }

Deep Run; brook in Buena Vista and Hamilton townships, Atlantic County, flows into Great Egg Harbor River ..... Hammonton.

Deep Run; brook in Alloway and Quinton townships, Salem County, tributary to Alloways Creek .... Salem.

Deep Run; brook in Marlboro Township, Monmouth County, and Madison Township, Middlesex County, flows into South River .... New Brunswick.

Deepavaal; brook in Caldwell Township, Essex County, tributary to Passic River .... Morristown.

Deepwater; point projecting from Lower Penns Neck Township, Salem County, into Delaware River .... Wilmington.

Deerfield; township in Cumberland County; area, 41 square miles. { Bridgeton. Bayside. Glassboro. }

Deerfield; village in Deerfield Township, Cumberland County. Glassboro.

Delair Station; village in Stockton Township, Camden County, on Pennsylvania R. R .... Philadelphia.

Delanco; village in Beverly Township, Burlington County, on Delaware River, and on Amboy Division, Pennsylvania R. R .... Burlington.

Delawanna; village in Acquackanonck Township, Passaic County, on Boonton Branch of Delaware, Lackawanna and Western R. R .... Paterson.

Delaware; township in Hunterdon County; area, 43 square miles. { Doylestown. Lambertville. High Bridge. }

Delaware; township in Camden County; area, 24 square miles. { Mount Holly. Philadelphia. }

Delaware; village in Knowlton Township, Warren County, on Delaware River, on Delaware, Lackawanna and Western R. R., and on New York, Susquehanna and Western R. R .... Delaware Water Gap.

Delaware and Raritan; canal connecting New Brunswick and Trenton, thence follows the Delaware River as far as Lambertville. { Plainfield. Somerville. Princeton. Bordentown. Burlington. Lambertville. }

Delaware Bay and Cape May; railroad running along shore of Lower Township, Cape May County, connecting with West Jersey R. R .... Cape May.

Dellett; village in Shamong Township, Burlington County. Mount Holly.

Delran; township in Burlington County; area, 9 square miles. { Burlington. Mount Holly. }

Demarest; village in Harrington Township, Bergen County, on Tienekill Creek, and on Northern R. R. of New Jersey. Harlem.

Den; brook rising in Randolph Township, flows into Rockaway River in Rockaway Township, Morris County. { Morristown. Lake Hopatcong. }

Denmark; village in Rockaway Township, Morris County, on Morris County R. R .... Lake Hopatcong.

Denmark; pond in Rockaway Township, Morris County .... Lake Hopatcong.

Names of sheets.

Denn Branch; brook in Stow Creek Township, Cumberland County, flows into Stow Creek .... Bayside.

Dennis; township in Cape May County; area, 68 square { Tuckahoe. miles. { Dennisville.

Dennis; creek in Dennis Township, Cape May County, flows into Delaware Bay at boundary line between Dennis and Middle townships.. Dennisville.

Dennisville; village in Dennis Township, Cape May County.. Dennisville.

Dentdale Station; village in Center Township, Camden County, on Philadelphia and Reading R. R............... Philadelphia.

Denville; village in Rockaway Township, on Rockaway River, and on Delaware, Lackawanna and Western R. R., and Boonton Branch of same road.......................... Morristown.

Deptford; township in Gloucester County; area, 20 square miles .... Philadelphia.

Devil; brook in South Brunswick Township, Middlesex County, tributary to Millstone River....... .... Princeton.

Devil's Hole; hill in Hampton Township, Sussex County; elevation, 620 feet... Wallpack.

Dias; creek in Middle Township, Cape May County, flows into Delaware Bay... Dennisville.

Dias Creek; village in Middle Township, Cape May County.. Dennisville.

Dick; brook in Howell Township, Monmouth County, flows into North Branch of Metedeconk River................... Asbury Park.

Dickerson; point of land projecting from Roxbury Township, Morris County, into Lake Hopatcong..................... Lake Hopatcong.

Dicktown; village in Winslow Township, Camden County.. Mount Holly.

Dildine; island off coast of Oxford Township, Warren County, in Delaware River............. .... Delaware Water Gap.

Dilkesboro; village in Mantua Township, Gloucester County. Glassboro.

Dilts Corner; village in Delaware Township, Hunterdon County... Lambertville.

Dinner; point projecting from Eagleswood Township, Ocean County, into Little Egg Harbor.......................... Little Egg Harbor.

Dinner Point; creek in Eagleswood Township, Ocean County, flows into Little Egg Harbor.......................... Little Egg Harbor.

Dismal; swamp in Piscataway and Raritan Townships, Middlesex County.. Plainfield.

Dividing; creek in Commercial and Downe Townships, Cum- } Bridgeton. berland County, forming partial boundary between the > two Townships, flows into Maurice River Cove. } Maurice Cove.

Dividing Creek; station in Downe Township, Cumberland County, on Central R. R. of New Jersey................. Bridgeton.

Dividing Creek; village in Downe Township, Cumberland County .... Bridgeton.

Division; creek in Fairfield Township, Cumberland County, flows into Middle Marsh Creek.......................... Bayside.

Division; creek in North Bergen Township, Hudson County, tributary to Hackensack River........................... Paterson.

Dixon; pond in Rockaway Township, Morris County....... Morristown.

Daniel Branch; brook in Lacey Township, Ocean County, tributary to Factory Branch .... Whitings.

Dark Branch; brook in Jackson Township, Ocean County, flows into Maple Root Branch.......................... Cassville.

Names of sheets.

Davenport; village in Berkeley Township, Ocean County, on Philadelphia and Long Branch R. R., and on Davenport Branch of Toms River. } Whitings. Barnegat.

Davenport; brook in Manchester and Berkeley Townships, Ocean County, tributary to Toms River. } Whitings. Barnegat.

Davisville; village in Jackson Township, Ocean County.... Cassville.

Decons; pond in Woodland Township, Burlington County .. Whitings.

Disbrow; hill in Millstone Township, Monmouth County; elevation, 268 feet............................... Cassville.

Dock Thorofare; passage in coast swamp in Egg Harbor Township, Atlantic County .... Great Egg Harbor.

Dock Watch Hollow; valley in Warren Township, Somerset County........................... Somerville.

Doctor; creek in Millstone and Upper Freehold townships, Monmouth County, and Hamilton Township, Mercer County, flows into Crosswick Creek. } Bordentown. Cassville.

Doctor; point projecting from Galloway Township, Atlantic County, into Mullica River............... Little Egg Harbor.

Dorchester; village in Maurice River Township, Cumberland County, on West Jersey R. R............... Tuckahoe.

Double Trouble; village in Berkeley Township, Ocean County, on Cedar Creek .... Barnegat.

Doughty; village in Galloway Township, Atlantic County .. Great Egg Harbor.

Doughty; village in Buena Vista Township, Atlantic County. Tuckahoe.

Doughty; creek in Galloway Township, Atlantic County, flows into Somer Cove .... Atlantic City.

Doughty Mill; village in Egg Harbor Township, Atlantic County .... Great Egg Harbor.

Dover; township in Ocean County; area, 56 square miles... } Barnegat. Asbury Park. Cassville.

Dover; town in Rockaway Township, Morris County, on Rockaway River, Morris Canal, on Delaware, Lackawanna and Western R. R., and on High Bridge Branch of Central R. R., of New Jersey............... Lake Hopatcong.

Dover Forge; village in Berkeley Township, Ocean County.. Whitings.

Downe; township in Cumberland County; area, 57 square miles. } Bridgetown. Maurice Cove.

Downer; village in Monroe Township, Gloucester County, on Philadelphia and Reading R. R............... Glassboro.

Downstown; village in Franklin Township, Gloucester County .... Hammonton.

Dunham Corners; village in East Brunswick Township, Middlesex County .... New Brunswick.

Drag; island in Great Egg Harbor in Egg Harbor Township, Atlantic County .... Great Egg Harbor.

Dragston; village in Downe Township, Cumberland County. Bridgeton.

Drake; pond in Andover Township, Sussex County .... Franklin.

Drake; brook in Roxbury, Mount Olive, and Washington townships, Morris County, flows into South Branch of Raritan River............... Lake Hopatcong.

Drakestown; village in Washington Township, Morris County .... Hackettstown.

Drakesville; village in Roxbury Township, Morris County, on Morris Canal .... Lake Hopatcong.

Names of sheets.

Drea Hook; village in Readington Township, Hunterdon County .... High Bridge.

Driver Branch; brook in Hammonton Township, Atlantic { Hammonton.
County, flows into Cedar Branch of Great Swamp Branch } Mullica.

Drum Bed; an enlargement of Back Creek in Fairfield Township, Cumberland County.................................. Bayside.

Drum Thorofare; passage in coast swamp in Middle Township, Cape May County .... Dennisville.

Drumbo; creek in Fairfield Township, Cumberland County, flows into Delaware River................................. Bayside.

Duck; island in Delaware River in Hamilton Township, Mercer County .... Bordentown.

Duck Pond; run in West Windsor Township, Mercer County, tributary to Stony Brook.................................... Princeton.

Dudley Station; village in Stockton Township, Camden County, on Pennsylvania R. R., Amboy division........... Philadelphia.

Dukes Bridge; village in Woodland Township, Burlington County .... Pemberton.

Duncan; island off coast of Linden Township, Union County, in Arthur Kill .... Staten Island.

Dundee Lake; village in Saddle River Township, Bergen County, on Passaic River, and on New York, Susquehanna and Western R. R.. Paterson.

Dunellen; borough in Middlesex County, on Green Brook, and on Central R. R. of New Jersey .... Plainfield.

Dung Thorofare; passage in coast swamp in Middle Township, Cape May County.................................... Dennisville.

Dunker; pond in West Milford Township, Passaic County... Greenwood Lake.

Dunnfield; village in Pahaquarry Township, Warren County, on Delaware River, and on Delaware, Lackawanna and Western R. R.. Delaware Water Gap.

Dunnfield; creek in Pahaquarry Township, Warren County, tributary to Delaware River............................. Delaware Water Gap.

Durham; pond in Rockaway Township, Morris County ..... Morristown.

Dutch Neck; village in West Windsor Township, Mercer County... Princeton.

Dutch Neck; high land in Hopewell Township, Cumberland County... Bridgeton.

Dyer; cove projecting from Delaware River into Downe Township, Cumberland County............................. Bridgeton.

Dyer; creek in Downe Township, Cumberland County, flows into Delaware River .... Bridgeton.

Eagle; point of land projecting from coast of West Deptford Township, Gloucester County, into Delaware River...... Philadelphia.

Eagle; village in Shamong Township, Burlington County... Pemberton.

Eagle; bay in coast swamp in Galloway Township, Atlantic County... Atlantic City.

Eagle Rock; village in West Orange Township, Essex County Paterson.

Eagleswood; township in Ocean County; area, 35 square { Little Egg Harbor.
miles. } Long Beach.

Eagleswood; village in Perth Amboy Township, Middlesex County, on Raritan River................................. Plainfield.

East; creek in Dennis Township, Cape May County, flows south into Delaware Bay.................................. Dennisville.

Names of sheets.

East; point projecting from coast of Maurice River Township, Cumberland County, into Maurice River Cove .... Maurice Cove.

East Amwell; township in Hunterdon County; area, 25 square miles.. Lambertville.

East Branch. *See* Oswego River.

East Brunswick; township in Middlesex County; area, 29 square miles.. New Brunswick.

East Camden; village in Stockton Township, Camden County, at junction of Amboy division with Pennsylvania R. R... Philadelphia.

East Creek; village in Dennis Township, Cape May County. Dennisville.

East Greenwich; township in Gloucester County; area, 14 square miles. { Chester. Philadelphia. }

East Lake; village in Pilesgrove Township, Salem County, on Salem Creek.. Salem.

East Long Branch; village in Ocean Township, Monmouth County, on Atlantic Ocean and New York and Long Branch R. R.. Sandy Hook.

East Millstone; borough in Franklin Township, Somerset County, on Millstone River, and on Delaware and Raritan Canal, at terminus of Millstone Branch of Pennsylvania R. R. { Somerville. Princeton. }

East Orange; township in Essex County; area, 4 square miles. { Paterson. Staten Island. }

East Orange; village in East Orange Township, Essex County, on Morris and Essex Division of Delaware, Susquehanna and Western R. R.. Paterson.

East Point; channel in coast swamp in Galloway Township, Atlantic County.. Atlantic City.

East Windsor; township in Mercer County; area, 17 square miles. { New Brunswick. Cassville. Princeton. Bordentown. }

Easthampton; township in Burlington County; area, 6 square miles. { Burlington. Mount Holly. Bordentown. Pemberton. }

Eatontown; township in Monmouth County; area, 12 square miles .... Sandy Hook.

Eatontown; village in Eatontown Township, Monmouth County, at junction of two branches of New Jersey Southern R. R.. Sandy Hook.

Bayrstown; village in Lumberton Township, Burlington County, on South Branch of Rancocas Creek............. Mount Holly.

Echo Lake; village in West Milford Township, Passaic County .... Greenwood Lake.

Eddy; creek in Upper Township, Cape May County, tributary to Job Creek.. Great Egg Harbor.

Edgar; village in Woodbridge Township, Middlesex County, on Perth Amboy Branch Pennsylvania R. R .... Plainfield.

Edge; cove projecting from Little Egg Harbor into Little Egg Harbor Township, Burlington County..................... Little Egg Harbor.

Edgewater; village in Ridgefield Township, Bergen County, on Hudson River.. Harlem.

Names of sheets.

Edgewater Park; village in Burlington and Beverly townships, Burlington County, on Delaware River, and on Amboy Division Pennsylvania R. R .... Burlington.

Edinburg; village in West Windsor Township, Mercer County, on Assanpink Creek.. Princeton.

Edison; village in Sparta Township, Sussex County......... Franklin.

Edward; run in Mantua Township, Gloucester County, { Philadelphia. tributary to Mantua Creek.   { Glassboro.

Egg; island in coast swamp in Galloway Township, Atlantic County... Atlantic City.

Egg Harbor; township in Atlantic County; area, 112 square { Great Egg Harbor. miles.   { Atlantic City.

Egg Harbor; inlet projecting from Atlantic Ocean into Egg Harbor Township, Atlantic County........................ Atlantic City.

Egg Harbor; city in Atlantic County; area, 11 square miles.. Mullica.

Egg Island; light-house on coast of Downe Township, Cumberland County... Maurice Cove.

Egg Island; point projecting from coast of Egg Island into Delaware Bay .... Maurice Cove.

Eight Mile Branch; brook in Stafford Township, Ocean { Little Egg Harbor. County, flowing into Mill Creek.   { Whitings.

Elberon; village in Ocean Township, Monmouth County, on New York and Long Branch R. R......................... Sandy Hook.

Elbow; beacon in Newark Bay............................. Staten Island.

Elisha Branch; brook in Plumstead and Jackson townships, Ocean County, flows into Gum Branch.................... Cassville.

Elizabeth; city in Union County; area, 13 square miles..... Staten Island.

Elizabeth; river rising in Essex County, enters Union { Paterson. County and flows through Elizabeth City into Arthur { Staten Island. Kill.   { Plainfield.

Elizabethport; part of Elizabeth City, at junction of Elizabeth River with Arthur Kill, on Newark Branch of Central R. R. of New Jersey................................... Staten Island.

Ellis; island off Jersey City in New York Upper Bay .... Staten Island.

Ellisburg; village in Delaware Township, Camden County.. Philadelphia.

Ellisdale; village in New Hanover Township, Burlington County .... Bordentown

Elm; village in Winslow Township, Camden County, on New Jersey Southern R. R .... Hammonton.

Elmer; village in Pittsgrove Township, Salem County, on West Jersey R. R .... Glassboro.

Elmora; village in Union Township, Union County, on Central R.R. of New Jersey................................... Staten Island.

Elmwood Road; village in Eversham Township, Burlington County .... Mount Holly.

Elsinboro; township in Salem County; area, 13 square miles.. Salem.

Elsinboro; point projecting from Elsinboro Township, Salem County, into Delaware River............................. Wilmington.

Elsinboro Neck; peninsula extending from Elsinboro Township, Salem County, into Delaware River................. Wilmington.

Elwood; village in Mullica Township, Atlantic County, on Philadelphia and Reading R. R........................... Mullica.

Emmelville; village in Hamilton Township, Atlantic County. Tuckahoe.

Names of sheets.

Emmons Station; village in Stillwater Township, Sussex County, on Paulins Hill, and on New York, Susquehanna and Western R. R. .... Wallpack.

Englewood; township in Bergen County; area, 11 square miles. { Harlem. Paterson.

Englewood; village in Englewood Township, Bergen County, on Northern R. R. of New Jersey and on Overpeck Creek. Harlem.

English; creek in Egg Harbor Township, Atlantic County, flows into Great Egg Harbor River........................ Great Egg Harbor.

English Creek; landing in Egg Harbor Township, Atlantic County, on English Creek................................. Great Egg Harbor.

English Creek; village in Egg Harbor Township, Atlantic County, on West Jersey R. R............................. Great Egg Harbor.

Englishtown; village in Manalapan Township, Monmouth County, on Freehold and Jamesburg R. R................. New Brunswick.

Ephraim; swampy island in Lower Township, Cape May County .... Cape May.

Eruston; village in Sayreville Township, Middlesex County, on Camden and Amboy R. R............................... New Brunswick.

Essex; county in north part of the State; area, 130 square miles. { Morristown. Paterson. Staten Island. Plainfield.

Essex; village in Belleville Township, Essex County, on Passaic River and on Paterson and Newark Branch of New York, Lake Erie and Western R. R. .... Paterson.

Estellville; village in Weymouth Township, Atlantic County. Great Egg Harbor.

Everittstown; village in Alexandria Township, Hunterdon County .... Easton.

Evesboro; village in Evesham Township, Burlington County. Mount Holly.

Evesham; township in Burlington County; area, 30 square miles .... Mount Holly.

Evona; village; part of Plainfield City, Union County, on Central R. R. of New Jersey.............................. Plainfield.

Ewan Mills; village in Harrison Township, Gloucester County .... Glassboro.

Ewansville; station in Southampton Township, Burlington County, on Philadelphia and Long Branch R. R. .... Pemberton.

Ewing; township in Mercer County; area, 18 square miles.. { Lambertville. Burlington.

Ewing; village in Ewing Township, Mercer County........ Lambertville.

Ewing Neck; village in Maurice River Township, Cumberland County... Dennisville.

Ewingville; village in Ewing Township, Mercer County, on Shabakunk Creek... Lambertville

Extonville; village in Hamilton Township, Mercer County, on Crosswick Creek... Bordentown.

Factory Branch; brook in Lacey Township, Ocean County, tributary to Cedar Creek. { Whitings. Barnegat.

Fairfield; township in Cumberland County; area, 42 square miles. { Bridgeton. Bayside.

Fairfield; station in Howell Township, Monmouth County, on Freehold and Jamesburg R. R. (Pennsylvania R. R.) .. Asbury Park.

Fairfield; village in Howell Township, Monmouth County.. Asbury Park.

Names of sheets

Fairfield; village in northern part of Caldwell Township, Essex County.. Morristown.

Fairhaven; village in Shrewsbury Township, Monmouth County, on Navesink River .... Sandy Hook.

Fairhaven; village in Saddle River Township, Bergen County. Paterson.

Fairmount; village in Tewksbury Township, Hunterdon County .... High Bridge.

Fairmount; village in Midland Township, Bergen County, on New Jersey and New York R. R............................ Paterson.

Fairton; village in Fairfield Township, Cumberland County, on Cohansey Creek .... Bridgeton.

Fairview; village in South Harrison Township, Gloucester County.. Glassboro.

Fairview; village in Ridgefield Township, Bergen County, on Northern R. R. of New Jersey.......................... Paterson.

Fairview; village in Deptford Township, Gloucester County. Philadelphia.

Fairview; village in Delran Township, Burlington County.. Burlington.

Fairview; village in Medford Township, Burlington County. Mount Holly.

Fairview; village in Middletown Township, Monmouth County .... Sandy Hook.

False Egg Island; point projecting from coast of Downe Township, Cumberland County, into Delaware Bay...... Maurice Cove.

Fanwood; township in Union County; area, 10 square miles. Plainfield.

Fanwood; village in Fanwood Township, Union County, on Central R. R. of New Jersey........................... Plainfield.

Farmersville; village in Tewksbury Township, Hunterdon County .... High Bridge.

Farmingdale; village in Howell Township, Monmouth County, on Freehold and Jamesburg R. R. and the New Jersey Southern R. R .... Asbury Park.

Feather Bed; brook in Woodland, Shamong, and Randolph townships, Burlington County, tributary to Talepehauken Brook. } Pemberton. Mullica.

Febletown; village in Hope Township, Warren County.... Hackettstown.

Fellowship; village in Mount Laurel Township, Burlington County .... Mount Holly.

Feltville; village in New Providence Township, Union County... Plainfield.

Fenwick; creek in Mannington Township, Salem County, flows into Salem Creek...................................... Salem.

Fenwick; village in Pilesgrove Township, Salem County ... Salem.

Ferro Mont; village in Randolph Township, Morris County, on Chester Branch of Delaware, Lackawanna and Western R. R.. Lake Hopatcong.

Fiddler; creek in Hopewell Township, Mercer County, tributary to Delaware River................................. Lambertville.

Fieldsboro; village in Bordentown Township, Burlington County, on Delaware River and on Pennsylvania R. R... Bordentown.

Fieldville; village in Piscataway Township, Middlesex County, on Raritan River................................ Somerville.

Findern; village in Bridgewater Township, Somerset County, on Central R. R. of New Jersey.......................... Somerville.

Finesville; village in Pohatcong Township, Warren County, on Musconetcong River .... Easton.

Finley; station in Deerfield Township, on West Jersey R. R. Bridgeton.

Names of sheets.

Finns; point projecting from Lower Penns Neck Township, Salem County, into Delaware River .... Wilmington.

First; river tributary to Passaic River flowing through Newark City, Essex County. { Staten Island. Paterson.

First Watchung; the outlying ridge of the Appalachian Mountains, runs through Passaic and Essex, Union and Somerset counties. { Paterson. Morristown. Plainfield. Somerville.

Fish Factory; village in Egg Harbor Township, Atlantic County, on Great Egg Harbor.............................. Great Egg Harbor.

Fish House Station; village in Stockton Township, Camden County, on Delaware River and on Pennsylvania R. R .. Philadelphia.

Fishing; creek rising in Middle Township, flowing southwesterly, passing through northwest corner of Lower Township, Cape May County, into Delaware Bay......... Dennisville.

Fishing; creek in Lower Alloways Creek Township, Salem County, flows into Stony Inlet.............................. Bayside.

Fishing; creek in Greenwich Township, Cumberland County, flows into Delaware River.................................. Bayside.

Fishing; creek, passage in coast swamp in Downe Township, Cumberland County....................................... Maurice Cove.

Fishing Creek; village in Middle township, Cape May County .... Dennisville.

Five Acre; pond near central part of Weymouth township, Atlantic County .... Tuckahoe.

Fivemile; beach along coast of Lower and Middle townships, Cape May County................................. Cape May.

Five Points; station on Philadelphia and Reading R. R., in Harrison Township, Gloucester County.................. Glassboro.

Flagtown (Frankfort, P. O.); village in Hillsboro Township, Somerset County...................................... Somerville.

Flanders; village in Mount Olive Township, Morrison County, on Drakes Brook and on High Bridge Branch of Central R. R., of New Jersey. .... Lake Hopatcong.

Flat; island in Little Egg Harbor, Stafford Township, Ocean County... Long Beach.

Flat; creek, passage in coast swamp in Stafford Township, Ocean County, flows into Manahawken Bay.............. Long Beach.

Flat; creek in Raritan and Holmdel Townships, Monmouth County, flows into Raritan Bay.......................... Sandy Hook.

Flat; creek in Upper Township, Cape May County, flows into Tuckahoe River... Great Egg Harbor.

Flat; brook formed by two branches, Little Flat and Big Flat Brooks; is in Sandstone and Wallpack townships, Sussex County, and flows into Delaware River .... Wallpack.

Flat Creek; passage in coast swamp in Upper Township, Cape May County....................................... Sea Isle.

Flatbrookville; village in Wallpack Township, Sussex, County, on Delaware River .... Wallpack.

Flemington; town in Raritan Township, Hunterdon County, on Flemington Branch Lehigh Valley R. R., on South Branch R. R. and on Flemington Branch of Belvidere Division, Pennsylvania R. R .... High Bridge.

Names of sheets.

Flemington Junction; village in Raritan Township, Hunterdon County, at junction of Flemington Branch with Lehigh Valley R. R.. High Bridge.

Florence; township in Burlington County; area, 10 square miles.. Burlington.

Florence; village in Winslow Township, Camden County, on Philadelphia and Reading R. R............................ Hammonton.

Florence; village in Florence Township, Burlington County. Burlington.

Florida Grove; village in Woodbridge Township, Middlesex County, on Raritan River................................... Plainfield.

Flyat; village in Shamong Township, Burlington County... Mount Holly.

Ford Corners; village in Raritan and Woodbridge townships, Middlesex County, on Lehigh Valley R. R................. Plainfield.

Fordville; village in Bridgeton Township, Cumberland County.. Bridgeton.

Forest Grove; village in Franklin Township, Gloucester County.. Hammonton.

Forked; river heading in three branches, North, Middle and South Branches, flows through Ocean County into Barnegat Bay. } Whitings. Barnegat.

Forked Branch; brook in Manchester Township, Ocean County, tributary to Old Hurricane Brook............... Whitings.

Forked River; hills in Lacey Township, Ocean County; elevation, 150, 180, 170 and 182 feet, respectively......... Whitings.

Forked River; village in Lacey Township, Oceon County, on New Jersey Southern R. R................................ Barnegat.

Forked River; life-saving station on Island Beach in Lacey Township, Ocean County................................ Barnegat.

Formosa Bogs; marsh in Upper Township, Cape May County.. Dennisville.

Fort Lee; town in Ridgefield Township, Bergen County, on Hudson River .... Harlem.

Fortesque; creek in Downe Township, Cumberland County, flows into Delaware Bay.................................... Maurice Cove.

Fortesque; village on coast of Downe Township, Cumberland County .... Maurice Cove.

Fortesque Neck; peninsula in coast swamp in Downe Township, Cumberland County................................. Bridgeton.

Foster Run; brook in Deerfield Township, Cumberland County; flows into Cohansey Creek. } Bridgeton. Bayside.

Fostertown; village in Lumberton Township, Burlington County .... Mount Holly.

Foulertown; brook in Livingston Township, Essex County, tributary to Passaic River .... Morristown.

Fountain Green; village in New Hanover Township, Burlington County .... Bordentown.

Fourmile; village in Woodland Township, Burlington County Pemberton.

Fourmile Branch; brook on boundary between Winslow Township, Camden County, and Monroe Township, Gloucester County; flows into Great Egg Harbor River ...... Hammonton.

Fourmile Branch; brook in Stafford Township, Ocean County; flows into Mill Creek. } Little Egg Harbor. Whitings.

Fox; hill in Washington Township, Morris County, and Tewksbury Township, Hunterdon County; greatest elevation being 1,026 feet .... High Bridge.

Names of sheets.

Fox Chase; village in Southampton and Shamong townships, Burlington County.. Pemberton.

Francis Mills; village in Jackson Township, Ocean County. Cassville.

Frankford; township in Sussex County; area, 37 square miles. { Wallpack. Franklin.

Franklin; township in Warren County; area, 24 square miles. { Delaware Water Gap. Easton. High Bridge.

Franklin; township in Hunterdon County; area, 23 square miles .... High Bridge.

Franklin; township in Gloucester County; area, 58 square miles. { Hammonton. Glassboro.

Franklin; township in Essex County; area, 3 square miles .. Paterson.

Franklin; township in Somerset County; area, 47 square miles. { Somerville. Plainfield. New Brunswick. Princeton.

Franklin; township in Bergen County; area, 29 square miles { Ramapo. Paterson. Morristown. Greenwood Lake.

Franklin; village in Franklin Township, Essex County, on Paterson and Newark Branch of New York, Lake Erie and Western R. R .... Paterson.

Franklin; village in Caldwell Township, Essex County..... Morristown.

Franklin; village in Rockaway Township, Morris County, on Delaware, Lackawanna and Western R. R............... Lake Hopatcong.

Franklin; lake in Franklin Township, Bergen county....... Paterson.

Franklin Corner; village in Lawrence Township, Mercer County, on Delaware and Raritan Canal and on Shipetau-kin Creek .... Princeton.

Franklin Furnace; village in Hardiston Township, Sussex County, on Sussex R. R .... Franklin.

Franklin Junction; village in Hardiston Township, Sussex County .... Franklin.

Franklin Park; village in South Brunswick Township, Middlesex County .... Princeton.

Franklin Park; village in North Brunswick Township, Middlesex County, on Pennsylvania R. R..................... New Brunswick.

Franklinville; village in Franklin Township, Gloucester County, on West Jersey R. R.............................. Glassboro.

Fredon; village in Stillwater Township, Sussex County..... Wallpack.

Freehold; township in Monmouth County; area, 41 square miles. { Cassville. Asbury Park. New Brunswick.

Freehold; town in Freehold Township, Monmouth County, at junction of Freehold and Jamesburg and Freehold and New York railroads....................................... New Brunswick.

Frelinghuysen; township in Warren County; area, 24 square miles. { Wallpack. Hackettstown.

Frenchtown; borough in Hunterdon County, on Delaware River, at junction of Nishisakawick Creek, and on Pennsylvania R. R., Belvidere Division .... Easton.

Names of sheets.

Fresh Ponds; village in South Brunswick Township, Middle-
sex County .... New Brunswick.

Friendship; creek in Woodland, Shamong, and Southampton
townships, Burlington County; flows into Cedar Run.... Pemberton.

Friendship; village in Upper Pittsgrove Township, Salem
County .... Glassboro.

Friendship; village in Deerfield Township, Cumberland
County .... Bridgeton.

Friendship; village in Woodland Township, Burlington
County, on Friendship Creek............................... Pemberton.

Friendship Bogs; village in Randolph Township, Burlington
County .... Mullica.

Fries Mills; village in Maurice River Township, Cumberland ·
County, on Manumuskin River............................... Tuckahoe.

Fries Mills; village in Franklin Township, Gloucester County. Glassboro.

Friesburg; village in Alloways Township, Salem County.... Salem.

Fruit Growers Union; village in Hammonton Township, Camden County.. Hammonton.

Furnace; brook in Oxford Township, Warren County, tribu- ⎧ Delaware Water Gap.
tary to Pequest River.   ⎩ Hackettstown.

Galloway; township in Atlantic County; area, 136 square
miles.

⎧ Great Egg Harbor.
⎨ Little Egg Harbor.
⎪ Mullica.
⎩ Atlantic City.

Game; creek in Oldmans and Upper Penns Neck townships,
Salem County; flows into Salem Creek.................... Salem.

Gander; brook in Manalapan Township, Monmouth County; ⎧ New Brunswick.
flows into Still House Brook.   ⎩ Cassville.

Garfield; town in Saddle River Township, Bergen County,
at junction of Saddle and Passaic rivers, and on New
York, Lake Erie and Western R. R .... Paterson.

Garret; hill in Middletown Township, Monmouth County;
elevation, 208 feet.. Sandy Hook.

Garret Rock; hill south of Paterson City, Passaic County;
altitude, 490 feet... Paterson.

Garton; village in Deerfield Township, Cumberland County,
on New Jersey Southern R. R............................... Bridgeton.

Gaskin Branch; brook in Jackson Township, Ocean County;
flows into Toms River... Cassville.

Gates Branch; brook in Woodland and Randolph town- ⎫ Pemberton.
ships, Burlington County, tributary to West Branch of ⎬ Mullica.
Wading River.   ⎭

Gaunt; brook in Manchester Township, Ocean County, and ⎫ Whitings.
Pemberton Township, Burlington County, tributary to ⎬ Pemberton.
Cranberry Brook.   ⎭

Genesis; bay in Middle Township, Cape May County, flowing
into Jenkins Sound .... Dennisville.

Georgetown; village in Mansfield Township, Burlington
County, on Bacon Run .... Bordentown.

Georgia; village in Freehold Township, Monmouth County.. Cassville.

German Valley; village in Washington Township, Morris
County, on South Branch of Raritan River and High
Bridge Branch of New Jersey Central R. R .... Hackettstown.

Names of sheets.

Germania; village in Galloway Township, Atlantic County, on Camden and Atlantic R. R............................. Mullica.

Germany Flats; valley in Sparta and Andover townships, Sussex County .... Franklin.

Gibbsboro; village in Waterford Township, Camden County. Mount Holly.

Gibbstown; village in Greenwich Township, Gloucester County, on Delaware River R. R .... Chester.

Giberson Mills; village in Manchester Township, Ocean County, on Wrangel Brook................................ Whitings.

Gibson; landing in Weymouth Township, Atlantic County, on Great Egg Harbor....................................... Great Egg Harbor.

Gibson; creek in Weymouth Township, Atlantic County; flows into Great Egg Harbor. { Tuckahoe. } Great Egg Harbor.

Gifford Mill Branch; brook in Little Egg Harbor Township, Burlington County, tributary to Tuckerton Creek........ Little Egg Harbor.

Gillette; village in Passaic Township, Morris County, on Passaic River and on Passaic and Delaware R. R .... Plainfield.

Gillmore; island in Barnegat Bay, off coast of Dover Township, Ocean County .... Barnegat.

Glades, The; marshy tract of land in Downe Township, Cumberland County... Bridgeton.

Glassboro; township in Gloucester County; area, 11 square miles .... Glassboro.

Glassboro; village in Glassboro Township, Gloucester County, on Philadelphia and Reading R. R.......................... Glassboro.

Glen Gardner; village in Lebanon Township, Hunterdon County, on Delaware, Lackawanna and Western R. R ... High Bridge.

Glen Ridge; village in Bloomfield Township, Essex County, on Bloomfield Branch of Delaware, Lackawanna and Western, and New York and Greenwood Lake R. Rs..... Paterson.

Glen Rock; village in Ridgewood Township, Bergen County, on New York, Lake Erie and Western R. R.............. Paterson.

Glendale; village in Waterford Township, Camden County. Mount Holly.

Glenmoore; village in Hopewell Township, Mercer County. Lambertville.

Glenwood; village in Vernon Township, Sussex County .... Goshen.

Gloucester; county in southwest part of State; area, 339 square miles. { Philadelphia. Chester. Salem. Glassboro. Hammonton. }

Gloucester; township in Camden County; area, 37 square miles. { Mount Holly. Philadelphia. Hammonton. }

Gloucester; city in Camden County, on Delaware River and on West Jersey R. R... Philadelphia.

Gloucester; village in Egg Harbor City, Atlantic County... Mullica.

Gloucester; lake in Egg Harbor City, Atlantic County, an enlargement of Indian Cabin Creek........................ Mullica.

Glover; pond in Frelinghuysen Township, Warren County.. Hackettstown.

Goffle; village in Manchester Township, Passaic County, on Goffle Brook .... Paterson.

Goffle; brook rising in Franklin Township, Bergen County; flows south through eastern part of Manchester Township, Passaic County, into Passaic River .... Paterson.

50   A GEOGRAPHIC DICTIONARY OF NEW JERSEY.

Gold; run in Ewing Township, Mercer County, tributary to Delaware River.. Lambertville.

Golden Thorofare; passage in coast swamp in Galloway Township, Atlantic County .... Atlantic City.

Good Intent; village in Deptford Township, Gloucester County, on South Branch of Timber Creek .... Philadelphia.

Goodluck; village in Lacey Township, Ocean County ...... Barnegat.

Goodluck; point of land projecting into coast swamp in Berkeley Township, Ocean County .... Barnegat.

Goodluck; island in Little Egg Harbor, in Little Egg Harbor Township, Burlington County .... Little Egg Harbor.

Goodwater; brook in Manchester Township, Ocean County, tributary to Old Hurricane Brook.......................... Whitings.

Goodwater Run; brook in Washington Township, Burlington County, flowing into Batsto River..................... Mullica.

Goodwater Run; brook in Woodland Township, Burlington County; flows into Governors Hill Brook. { Whitings. Pemberton.

Goose; pond in Manchester Township, Ocean County .... Whitings.

Goose; pond in Woodland Township, Burlington County ... Whitings.

Goose; creek in Dover Township, Ocean County; flows into into Barnegat Bay..., ... Barnegat.

Goshen; creek in Middle Township, Cape May County; flows into Delaware Bay.. Dennisville.

Goshen; landing in Middle Township, Cape May County, on Goshen Creek.. Dennisville.

Goshen; village in Middle Township, Cape May County .... Dennisville

Gouldtown; village in Bridgeton Township, Cumberland County.. Bridgeton

Governor Branch; brook in Bass River and Little Egg Harbor townships, Burlington County; flows into Westecunk Creek .... Little Egg Harbor.

Governors Hill; brook in Woodland Township, Burlington County, tributary to Gates Branch of Wading River .... Pemberton.

Granney; creek in Dennis Township, Cape May County, flowing into Main Channel............................... Sea Isle.

Granton; village in North Bergen Township, Hudson County. Paterson.

Grassy; bay in coast swamp in Galloway Township, Atlantic County... Atlantic City.

Grassy Sound; channel in Middle Township, Cape May County, connecting Dead Thorofare with Grassy Sound.. Dennisville.

Grassy; pond in Weymouth Township, Atlantic County.... Tuckahoe.

Grassy; sound in Middle and Lower townships, Cape May County. { Cape May. Dennisville.

Gravel Hill; village in Monroe Township, Middlesex County. New Brunswick.

Gravelly Run; brook in Downe and Millville townships, Cumberland County....................,................. Bridgeton.

Gravelly Run; village in Hamilton Township, Atlantic County .... Great Egg Harbor.

Gravelly Run; brook in Hamilton Township, Atlantic County; flows into Great Egg Harbor River.............. Great Egg Harbor.

Gravelly Run; passage in coast swamp in Middle Township, Cape May County... Dennisville.

Graven Thorofare; passage in coast swamp in Middle Township, Cape May County............................... Sea Isle.

Names of sheets.

Great; bay forming partial boundary between Little Egg Harbor Township, Burlington County, and Galloway Township, Atlantic County............................ Atlantic City.

Great; channel in Lower Township, Cape May County, connecting Heretford Inlet with Great Sound................ Dennisville.

Great; island in swamp east of Elizabeth City, Union County.. Staten Island.

Great; sound in Middle Township, Cape May County, flowing into Great Channel...................................... Dennisville.

Great; swamp in Hammonton Township, Atlantic County. { Hammonton. Mullica.

Great; swamp in Passaic and Chatham townships, Morris County... Plainfield.

Great Beds; light-house in Raritan Bay..................... New Brunswick.

Great Cedar; swamp in Dennis and Upper townships, Cape May County. { Dennisville. Great Egg Harbor. Sea Isle.

Great Ditch; brook in South Brunswick Township, Middlesex County, tributary to Lawrence Brook. { Princeton. New Brunswick.

Great Egg; harbor, an inlet of the Atlantic Ocean, on coast of Upper Township, Cape May County, and of Weymouth and Egg Harbor townships, Atlantic County .... Great Egg Harbor.

Great Egg; life-saving station on Absecon Beach .... Great Egg Harbor.

Great Egg Harbor; river rising in Gloucester Township, Camden County; flows on boundary between Camden and Burlington counties, then across Atlantic County into Great Egg Harbor. { Mount Holly. Great Egg Harbor. Hammonton.

Great Flat Thorofare; passage in coast swamp in Middle Township, Cape May County................................ Dennisville.

Great Notch; village in Little Falls Township, Passaic County, on New York and Greenwood Lake R. R .... Paterson.

Great Piece; meadows in Caldwell Township, Essex County. Morristown.

Great Swamp Branch; brook in Winslow Township, Camden County, and Hammonton Township, Atlantic County; flows into Nescochaque Creek. { Hammonton. Mullica.

Great Thorofare; passage in coast swamp in Egg Harbor Township, Atlantic County .... Atlantic City.

Great Thorofare; passage in coast swamp in Galloway Township, Atlantic County...................................... Atlantic City.

Greater Cross Roads; village in Bedminster Township, Somerset County, on Middle Brook....................... Somerville.

Green; township in Sussex County; area, 21 square miles .. { Wallpack. Hackettstown. Lake Hopatcong.

Green; brook, tributary to Raritan River, rises in North Plainfield Township, Somerset County, and forms boundary between Union, Middlesex, and Somerset counties. { Plainfield. Somerville.

Green (or **Lawrence**); brook in Maurice River Township, Cumberland County, flowing into Tuckahoe River .... Tuckahoe.

Green; brook in Dover and Brick townships, Ocean County, tributary to Kettle Creek .... Asbury Park.

Green; brook in Caldwell Township, Essex County, tributary to Deepavaal Brook................................... Morristown,

Names of sheets.

Green; mines in eastern part of Vernon Township, Sussex County ...... Greenwood Lake.

Green; creek in Middle Township, Cape May County, flowing into Delaware Bay ...... Dennisville.

Green; pond in Hope Township, Warren County ...... Hackettstown.

Green; pond in Rockaway Township, Morris County, on boundary of Jefferson Township.
{ Greenwood Lake.
Franklin.
Lake Hopatcong.
Morristown.

Green; village in Passaic Township, Morris County ...... Plainfield.

Green; village in Greenwich Township, Gloucester County, on Delaware River R. R. ...... Chester.

Green Bank; village on boundary line between Randolph and Washington townships, Burlington County ...... Mullica.

Green Branch; brook in Manchester Township, Ocean County, tributary to Wrangel Brook ...... Whitings.

Green Creek; village in Middle Township, Cape May County. Dennisville.

Green Grove; village in Shrewsbury Township, Monmouth County ...... Asbury Park.

Green Island; village in Dover Township, Ocean County, on Barnegat Bay ...... Asbury Park.

Green Pond; range of mountains extending along eastern boundary of Jefferson Township, Morris County.
{ Lake Hopatcong.
Franklin.
Greenwood Lake.

Green Pond; brook in Rockaway Township, Morris County, flows into Rockaway River ...... Lake Hopatcong.

Green Pond; mines in Rockaway Township, Morris County. Greenwood Lake.

Green Tree; village in Washington Township, Gloucester County ...... Philadelphia.

Greenland; village in Gloucester Township, Camden County. Philadelphia.

Greensville; village in Green Township, Sussex County .... Hackettstown.

Greenville; village in Pittsgrove Township, Salem County .. Glassboro.

Greenville; village in northern part of Rockaway Township, Morris County ...... Morristown.

Greenville; part of Jersey City on Hackensack River, on New York Upper Bay and on Central R. R. of New Jersey. Staten Island.

Greenwich; township in Warren County; area, 11 square miles ...... Easton.

Greenwich; township in Gloucester County; area, 15 square miles.
{ Chester.
Philadelphia

Greenwich; township in Cumberland County; area, 19 square miles ...... Bayside.

Greenwich; village in Greenwich Township, Cumberland County ...... Bayside.

Greenwood; lake extending into West Milford Township Passaic County, and into New York ...... Greenwood Lake.

Griggstown; village in Franklin Township, Somerset County, on Millstone River and on Delaware and Raritan Canal.. Princeton.

Gromakill; creek in North Bergen Township, Hudson County, tributary to Hackensack River ...... Paterson.

Ground Hog; brook in Howell Township, Monmouth County, flows into Polypod Brook ...... Asbury Park.

Grove Street; village in East Orange Township, Essex County, on Morris and Essex Division of Delaware, Lackawanna and Western R. R ...... Paterson.

Names of sheets.

Grovers Mill; village in West Windsor Township, Mercer
County, on Bear Brook.. Princeton.

Groverville; village in Hamilton Township, Mercer County,
on Crosswick Creek.. Bordentown.

Gulf; point projecting from Union Township, Ocean County,
into Barnegat Bay .... Long Beach.

Gull; swampy island in Middle Township, Cape May County,
surrounded by waters of Great Sound and Cresse Thoro-
fare .... Dennisville.

Gull Bar; marshy island in Hereford Inlet, in Middle Township, Cape May County...................................... Dennisville.

Gull Island Thorofare; passage in coast swamp in Galloway
Township, Atlantic County .... Atlantic City.

Gum; brook in Brick Township, Ocean County, flows into
Metedeconk River .... Asbury Park.

Gum Branch; brook in Plumstead and Jackson townships,
Ocean County, flows into Ridgway Branch.................... Cassville,

Gum Spring; brook tributary to Burrs Mill Brook, in Woodland Township, Burlington County .... Pemberton.

Gun Branch; brook in Waterford Township, Camden County,
and Hammonton Township, Atlantic County, tributary } Hamonton.
to Mechesactauxin Branch of Mullica River. } Mullica.

Gunning; river in coast swamp in Stafford and Union townships, Ocean County .... Long Beach.

Guttenberg; town in Hudson County, on Hudson River.... { Harlem.
{ Paterson.

Hackensack; town, coextensive with new Barbadoes Township, Bergen County, on Hackensack River and on New
Jersey and New York R. R.................................. Paterson.

Hackensack; river rising in Rockland County, runs south-
ward through Bergen and Hudson counties into Newark
Bay. { Tarrytown.
{ Ramapo.
{ Harlem.
{ Paterson.
{ Staten Island.

Hackettstown; town in Independence Township, Warren
County, on Musconetcong River and on Delaware, Lackawanna and Western R. R................................... Hackettstown.

Hacklebarney; village in Chester Township, Morris County,
on Black River and on Chester Branch of Delaware,
Lackawanna and Western R. R .... Lake Hopatcong.

Haddon; township in Camden County; area, 12 square miles. Philadelphia.

Haddonfield; borough in Haddon Township, Camden County,
on Camden and Atlantic R. R .... Philadelphia.

Hagerstown; village in Lower Alloways Creek Township,
Salem County .... Salem.

Hainesburg; village in Knowlton Township, Warren County,
on Paulins Kill and on New York, Susquehanna and West-
ern R. R... Delaware Water Gap.

Hainesport; village in Lumberton Township, Burlington
County, on Rancocas Creek and on Pennsylvania R. R... Mount Holly.

Hainesville; village in Sandyston Township, Sussex County,
on Little Flat Brook...................................... Milford.

Hakihokake; creek rising in Alexandria Township, flows
into Delaware River in southeast part of Holland Township, Hunterdon County .... Easton.

54   A GEOGRAPHIC DICTIONARY OF NEW JERSEY.

Names of sheets.

Haleyville; village in Commercial Township, Cumberland County. ... Bridgeton.

Half Acre; village in Monroe Township, Middlesex County. New Brunswick.

Halfway; creek in Upper Township, Cape May County, tributary to Cedar Swamp Creek ... Great Egg Harbor.

Haledon; village in Manchester Township, Passaic County, on Oldham Brook ... Paterson.

Halifax; village in Hohokus Township, Bergen County ... Ramapo.

Hall Run; brook in Mannington Township, Salem County, flows into Mannington Creek ... Salem.

Halltown; village in Mannington Township, Salem County, Salem.

Halsey; island off western coast of Jefferson Township, Morris County, and eastern coast Byram Township, Sussex County, in Lake Hopatcong ... Lake Hopatcong.

Ham; island in Little Egg Harbor, Eagleswood Township, Ocean County ... Long Beach.

Hamburg; town in Hardyston Township, Sussex County, on Walkill River and at junction of New York, Susquehanna and Western R. R. and Lehigh and Hudson River R.R... Franklin.

Hamden; village in Clinton Township, Hunterdon County, on South Branch of Raritan River and on Lehigh Valley R. R. High Bridge.

Hamilton; township in Mercer County; area, 41 square miles. { Princeton. Bordentown. Burlington.

Hamilton; township in Atlantic County; area, 114 square miles. { Hammonton. Mullica. Great Egg Harbor. Tuckahoe.

Hamilton Square; village in Hamilton Township, Mercer County ... Bordentown.

Hamilton Station; village in Hillsboro Township, Somerset County, on Philadelphia and Reading R. R ... Somerville.

Hammock; cove projecting from Little Bay, in Galloway Township, Atlantic County ... Atlantic City.

Hammonton; township in Atlantic County; area, 45 square miles ... Mullica.

Hammonton; town in Hammonton township, Atlantic County, on Camden and Atlantic R. R ... Hammonton.

Hammonton; creek in Hammonton and Mullica townships, Atlantic County, flows into Mullica River ... Mullica.

Hammon Branch; brook in Hammonton and Mullica townships, Atlantic County, flows into Hammonton Creek. { Hammonton. Mullica.

Hampton; township in Sussex County; area, 30 square miles { Wallpack. Franklin.

Hampton Furnace; village in Shamong Township, Burlington County ... Pemberton.

Hampton Gate; village in Shamong Township, Burlington County, on Batsto River ... Pemberton.

Hance Bridge; village in Landis Township, Cumberland County ... Tuckahoe.

Hancock Bridge; village in Lower Alloways Creek Township, Salem County ... Salem.

Hanks; pond in West Milford Township, Passaic County... Greenwood Lake.

Hanover; township in Morris County; area, 52 square miles { Morristown. Lake Hopatcong.

Names of sheets.

Hanover; station in Pemberton Township, Burlington County, on Philadelphia and Long Branch R. R. .... Pemberton.
Hanover; village in Hanover Township, Morris County..... Morristown.
Hanover Furnace; village in Pemberton Township, Burlington County .... Pemberton.
Hanover Neck; village in Hanover Township, Morris County. Morristown.
Hansey; creek in Commercial and Downe townships, Cumberland County, flows into Dividing Creek .... Maurice Cove.
Harbourton; village in Hopewell Township, Mercer County... Lambertville.
Hardenberg Corners; village in East Brunswick Township, Middlesex County .... New Brunswick.
Harding; village in Clayton Township, Gloucester County, on West Jersey R. R .... Glassboro.
Hardingville; village in Clayton Township, Gloucester County .... Glassboro.
Hardyston; township in Sussex County; area, 39 square miles. { Franklin. Greenwood Lake.
Hardystonville; village in Hardyston Township, Sussex County, on Walkill River, and on New York, Susquehanna and Western R. R.; also on Lehigh and Hudson River R. R .... Franklin.
Hardwick; township in Warren County; area, 18 square miles. { Wallpack. Hackettstown.
Hardwick; village in Hardwick Township, Warren County, on Blair Creek .... Wallpack.
Hardwick Center; village in Hardwick Township, Warren County, on Blair Creek .... Wallpack.
Harihokake; creek in Alexandria Township, Hunterdon County, tributary to the Delaware River .... Easton.
Harlingen; village in Montgomery Township, Somerset County .... Princeton.
Harmersville; village in Lower Alloways Creek Township, Salem County .... Bayside.
Harmony; township in Warren County; area, 24 square miles. { Delaware Water Gap. Easton.
Harmony; village in Hopewell Township, Cumberland County .... Salem.
Harmony; village in Harmony Township, Warren County, on Delaware River, and on Belvidere Division, Pennsylvania R. R .... Delaware Water Gap.
Harmony; village in Harmony Township, Warren County.. Easton.
Harrington; township in Bergen County; area, 27 square miles. { Tarrytown. Harlem. Paterson. Ramapo.
Harris; station in Woodland Township, Burlington County, on New Jersey Southern R. R .... Pemberton.
Harris Branch; brook in Jackson Township, Ocean County, flows into Ridgeway Branch .... Cassville.
Harrison; township in Gloucester County; area, 19 square miles. { Glassboro. Salem.
Harrison; town in Hudson County, on Passaic River....... { Paterson. Staten Island.
Harrison; brook in Bernard Township, Somerset County, tributary to Dead River .... Somerville.

Names of sheets.

Harrison Pond Branch; brook in Plumstead and Jackson townships, Ocean County, flows into Gum Branch .... Cassville.

Harrisonville; village in Lower Penns Neck Township, Salem County .... Salem.

Harrisonville; station in South Harrison Township, Gloucester County, on West Jersey R. R........................... Salem.

Harrisville; village in South Harrison Township, Gloucester County .... Salem.

Harrisville; village in Bass River Township, Burlington County, on Wading River... Mullica.

Harrow Run; brook in Deerfield Township, Cumberland { Glassboro. County, flows into Cohansey Creek........................ { Bayside.

Hartford; village in Mount Laurel Township, Burlington County, on Pennsylvania R.R .... Mount Holly.

Harvey Cedars; village on beach in Union Township, Ocean County, and on Long Beach R. R .... Long Beach.

Harvey Cedars; life saving station on coast of Union Township, Ocean County .... Long Beach.

Harvey Sedges; islands in Union Township, Ocean County, in Manahauken Bay .... Long Beach.

Hatfield; swamp along Passaic River in Livingston and Caldwell townships, Essex County .... Morristown.

Haven; point projecting from Brick Township, Ocean County, into Barnegat Bay .... Asbury Park

Haven; cove projecting from Barnegat Bay into Brick Township, Ocean County... Asbury Park.

Hawthorne; village in Manchester Township, Passaic County, on Passaic River, on New York, Lake Erie and Western R. R., and on New York, Susquehanna and Western R. R. Paterson.

Hay Cut; brook in Downe Township, Cumberland County, flows into Nantuxent Creek .... Bridgeton.

Hay Stack; brook in Howell Township, Monmouth County, flows into Metedeconk River .... Asbury Park.

Haynes; creek tributary to Rancocas Creek, in Medford and Lumberton Townships, Burlington County............... Mount Holly.

Hazen; post-office of Oxford Church, in Oxford Township, Warren County, on Pophandusing Brook .... Delaware Water Gap

Hazlet; village in Raritan Township, Monmouth County, on New York and Long Branch R. R .... Sandy Hook.

Head of River; village in Weymouth Township, Atlantic County, on Tuckahoe River.................................. Tuckahoe.

Headleytown; village in Union Township, Union County... Plainfield.

Headquarters; village in Delaware Township, Hunterdon County .... Lambertville.

Heard; brook in Woodbridge Township, Middlesex County, tributary to Woodbridge Creek............................ Plainfield.

Hedger House; village in Woodland Township, Burlington County .... Pemberton.

Heislerville; village in Maurice River Township, Cumberland County .... Dennisville.

Helmetta; village in East Brunswick Township, Middlesex County, on Camden and Amboy R. R .... New Brunswick.

Hendersons; cove, an arm of Lake Hopatcong indenting coast between Byram Township, Sussex County, and Jefferson township, Morris County.............................. Lake Hopatcong.

Names of sheets.

Hendricks; island off coast of Delaware Township, Hunterdon County, in Delaware River. { Doylestown. / Lambertville.

Hensfoot; village in Union Township, Hunterdon County ... High Bridge.

Herbertsville; village in Brick Township, Ocean County.. Asbury Park.

Hereford; inlet extending from the Atlantic Ocean into coast of Middle Township, Cape May County .... Dennisville.

Hereford; light-house on coast of Middle Township, Cape May County .... Dennisville.

Hereford Inlet; life saving-station on coast of Middle Township, Cape May County .... Dennisville.

Herman; village in Washington Township, Burlington County, on Bull Creek .... Mullica.

Herring; island in Metedeconk River, in Brick Township, Ocean County .... Asbury Park.

Hesstown; village in Maurice River Township, Cumberland County .... Tuckahoe.

Hetty; creek in Middle Township, Cape May County, flowing into Genesis Bay... Dennisville.

Hewett; village in West Milford Township, Passaic County, on Wanaque River and on New York and Greenwood Lake R. R .... Greenwood Lake.

Hewitt; pond in Andover Township, Sussex County .... Franklin.

Hewittville; village in Galloway Township, Atlantic County { Great Egg Harbor. / Atlantic City.

Hibernia; village in Rockaway Township, Morris County, on Hibernia Brook and on Hibernia Mine R. R............... Morristown.

Hibernia; brook in Rockaway Township, Morris County, tributary to Beaver Brook. { Morristown. / Lake Hopatcong.

Higbee; landing on coast of Lower Township, Cape May County .... Cape May.

Higbeeville; village in Galloway Township, Atlantic County. Little Egg Harbor.

High; island in Little Egg Harbor in Stafford Township, Ocean County .... Long Beach.

High; mountain in Manchester Township, Passaic County; altitude, 879 feet .... Paterson.

High Bank; landing on Great Egg Harbor River in Weymouth Township, Atlantic County .... Great Egg Harbor.

High Bridge; township in Hunterdon County; area, 18 square miles .... High Bridge.

High Bridge; village in High Bridge Township, Hunterdon County, on South Branch of Raritan River at junction of Delaware, Lackawanna and Western R. R. with High Bridge Branch of Central R. R. of New Jersey and the Central R. R. of New Jersey .... High Bridge.

High Point; mountain in Montague and Wantage Townships, Sussex County; altitude, 1,809 feet..................... Port Jervis.

Highland Beach; village in Middletown Township, Monmouth County .... Sandy Hook.

Highland Park; town in Raritan Township, Middlesex County, on Raritan River and on Pennsylvania R. R...... New Brunswick.

Highlands; village on reef in Middletown Township, Monmouth County, on New York and Long Branch R. R..... Sandy Hook.

Highlands of Navesink; hills in Middleton Township, Monmouth County; highest summit, 275 feet.................. Sandy Hook.

Names of sheets.

Hightstown; borough in Mercer County, on Millstone River and on Pennsylvania R. R., Amboy division .... Princeton.

Highwood; village in Englewood and Palisade townships, Bergen County, on Northern R. R. of New Jersey........ Harlem.

Hill Crest; village in Ewing Township, Mercer County, on Trenton branch, New York Division, Philadelphia and Reading R. R. .... Burlington.

Hillsboro; Township in Somerset County; area 58 square miles.
{ High Bridge.
Lambertville.
Princeton.
Somerville.

Hillsboro; village in Hillsboro Township, Somerset County, on Lehigh Valley R. R.
{ Princeton.
Somerville.

Hillsdale; village in Marlboro Township, Monmouth County. Sandy Hook.

Hillsdale; village in Washington Township, Bergen County, on Pascack Creek and on New Jersey and New York R. R. Ramapo.

Hither; island in Little Egg Harbor, in Little Egg Harbor Township, Burlington County............................. Little Egg Harbor.

Hilton; village in South Orange and Clinton Townships, Essex County.
{ Staten Island.
Plainfield.

Hoboken; city in Hudson County, on Hudson River, north of Jersey City.
{ Paterson.
Staten Island.

Hockamick; village in New Hanover Township, Burlington County, on South Run .... Bordentown.

Hockhockson; swamp in Atlantic Township, Monmouth County.. Sandy Hook.

Hockhockson; brook in Atlantic Township, Monmouth County, tributary to Pine Brook .... Sandy Hook.

Hoffman; station on Freehold and Jamesburg R. R., in Monroe Township, Middlesex County .... New Brunswick.

Hog; islands in Mullica River, in Randolph Township, Burlington County .... Mullica.

Hohokus; creek rising in Franklin Township, flows into Saddle River, in Ridgewood Township, Bergen County.
{ Ramapo.
Paterson.

Hohokus; township in Bergen County; area, 30 square miles. Ramapo.

Hohokus; village in Orvil Township, Bergen County, on Hohokus Creek and on New York, Lake Erie and Western R. R... Ramapo.

Holcombe; island off coast of Hunterdon County, opposite Lambertville City, in Delaware River .... Lambertville.

Holland; township in Hunterdon County; area, 25 square miles.. Easton.

Holland; village in Hardyston Township, Sussex County.... Franklin.

Holland Station; village in Holland Township, Hunterdon County, on Delaware River and on Pennsylvania R. R., Belvidere Division...................................... Easton.

Holland; brook rising in Readington Township, Hunterdon County, flows into South Branch of Raritan River, in Branchburg Township, Somerset County.
{ Somerville.
High Bridge.

Holly Beach; borough in Lower Township, Cape May County. Cape May.

Holly Beach; life-saving station on coast of Lower Township, Cape May County .... Cape May.

Holmansville; village in Jackson Township, Ocean County, on Toms River .... Cassville.

A GEOGRAPHIC DICTIONARY OF NEW JERSEY. 59

Names of sheets.

Holmdel; township in Monmouth County; area 18 square miles ... Sandy Hook.

Holmdel; village in Holmdel Township, Monmouth County. Sandy Hook.

Home Run; brook in Mannington Township, Salem County, flows into Salem Creek... Salem.

Hominy; hills in Atlantic Township, Monmouth County.... Sandy Hook.

Honey; branch of Stony Brook in Hopewell Township, Mercer County. { Lambertville. Princeton.

Honey Run; brook rising in Knowlton Township, Warren County, flows east into Beaver Brook in Hope Township, Warren County. { Delaware Water Gap. Hackettstown.

Hook; beacon at north end of Sandy Hook ... Sandy Hook.

Hook; brook in Millville Township, Cumberland County, flows into Manumuskin Creek... Tuckahoe.

Hop; brook tributary to Swimming River, forms partial boundary between Middletown and Holmdel townships on the north and Atlantic Township, Monmouth County, on the south ... Sandy Hook.

Hopatcong; lake in Morris County, touching southeast border of Sussex County. It forms boundary between Roxbury and Jefferson townships, Morris County, and Byram Township, Sussex County... Lake Hopatcong.

Hope; township in Warren County; area 31 square miles. { Delaware Water Gap. Hackettstown.

Hope; village in Hope Township, Warren County, on Beaver Brook ... Hackettstown.

Hopeville; village in Wall Township, Monmouth County ... Asbury Park.

Hopewell; township in Mercer County; area, 60 square miles. { Lambertville. Princeton.

Hopewell; township in Cumberland County; area, 34 square miles. { Bridgeton. Bayside. Salem.

Hopewell; village in Sparta Township, Sussex County... Franklin.

Hopewell; village in Hopewell Township, Mercer County, on New York Division, Philadelphia and Reading R. R... Lambertville.

Hopping; village in Middletown Township, Monmouth County, on Atlantic Highlands Branch of New Jersey Southern R. R ... Sandy Hook.

Horicon; village in Manchester Township, Ocean County ... Whitings.

Hornerstown; village in Upper Freehold Township, Monmouth County, on Pemberton and Hightstown R. R... Bordentown.

Horse; point projecting from Little Egg Harbor into Eagleswood Township, Ocean County... Little Egg Harbor.

Horse Neck Bridge; village in Montville Township, Morris County, on Passaic River... Morristown.

Horse Run; brook forming partial boundary between Stow Creek Township, Cumberland County, and Quinton and Lower Alloways Creek Townships, Salem County, flows into Stow Creek ... Bayside.

Horton; village in Chester Township, Morris County, on Chester Branch of Delaware, Lackawanna and Western R. R... Lake Hopatcong.

Names of sheets.

Hospitality; brook in Randolph Township, Burlington County, flows into Little Hauken .... Mullica.

Hospitality Branch; brook rising in Monroe Township, Gloucester County, flows through Monroe Township and across Buena Vista Township, Atlantic County, into Great Egg Harbor River. } Hammonton. Glassboro.

Houtenville; village in Woodbridge Township, Middlesex County, on South Branch of Rahway River and on Pennsylvania R. R .... Plainfield.

Howardsville; village in Lacey Township, Ocean County.. Whitings.

Howell; township in Monmouth County; area, 66 square miles... { Asbury Park. Cassville. Sandy Hook.

Howell; village in Howell Township, Monmouth County.. Cassville.

Howell; creek in Lawrence Township, Cumberland County, flows into Cedar Creek................................ Bridgeton.

Howell; station in Howell Township, Monmouth County, on Freehold and Jamesburg R. R., Pennsylvania R. R...... Asbury Park.

Howell; pond in Andover Township, Sussex County .... Franklin.

Hubbard; creek in Upper Township, Cape May County, flows into Peck Bay .... Great Egg Harbor.

Huckleberry Hill; village in Southampton Township, Burlington County .... Pemberton.

Hudson; county in northeast part of the State; area, 60 square miles. { Paterson. Harlem. Staten Island.

Hudson; river rising in the Adirondack Mountains of New York, flows south into New York Bay. { Tarrytown. Harlem. Paterson. Staten Island.

Hughes; creek in Upper Township, Cape May County, flows into Tuckahoe River... Great Egg Harbor.

Hughesville; village in Pohatcong Township, Warren County, on Musconetcong River and on Lehigh Valley R. R...... Easton.

Hunt; pond in Green Township, Sussex County............. Wallpack.

Hunterdon; county in northwest part of the State; area, 439 square miles. { Easton. Doylestown. Lambertville. High Bridge. Hackettstown. Somerville.

Hunters Mill; village in Weymouth Township, Atlantic County, on Tuckahoe River............................... Tuckahoe.

Huntsville; village in Green Township, Sussex County, on Lehigh and Hudson River R. R........................... Hackettstown.

Hurdtown; village in Jefferson Township, Morris County, on Weldon Brook and on the Central R. R. of New Jersey.. Lake Hopatcong.

Hurffville; village in Washington Township, Gloucester County... Philadelphia.

Husted; village in Deerfield Township, Cumberland County, on West Jersey R. R .... Glassboro.

Hutchinson; village in Harmony Township, Warren County, at junction of Buckhorn Creek with Delaware River and on Belvidere Division, Pennsylvania R. R................. Delaware Water Gap.

Names of sheets.

Iliff; pond in Andover Township, Sussex County .... Franklin.

Imlaystown; village in Upper Freehold Township, Monmouth County, on Doctor Creek .... Bordentown.

Independence; township in Warren County; area 20 square miles .... Hackettstown.

Independence Corner; village in Vernon Township, Sussex County .... Franklin.

India; brook in Randolph and Mendham townships, Morris County, tributary to North Branch of Raritan River..... Lake Hopatcong.

Indian; creek in Commercial Township, Cumberland County, tributary to Dividing Creek .... Maurice Cove.

Indian Branch; brook in Hamilton and Buena Vista townships, Atlantic County, flows into Great Egg Harbor River... Hammonton.

Indian Jack; brook in Woodland Township, Burlington County .... Whitings.

Indian Mills; village in Shamong Township, Burlington County, on Muskingum Brook............................. Pemberton.

Ingersoll Branch; brook in Maurice River Township, Cumberland County, flows west into Manumuskin River ..... Tuckahoe.

Indian Cabin; creek rising in Mullica Township; flows northeast through portion of Egg Harbor City, Atlantic County, into Mullica River .... Mullica.

Ingram Thorofare; passage in coast swamp in Middle Township, Cape May County..................................... Sea Isle.

Interlaken; village in Ocean Township, Monmouth County. Asbury Park.

Iona; village in Franklin Township, Gloucester County, on West Jersey R. R... Glassboro.

Iresick; brook in Madison Township, Middlesex County; flows into South River .... New Brunswick.

Ironia; village in Randolph Township, Morris County, on Chester Branch of Delaware, Lackawanna and Western R. R... Lake Hopatcong.

Irvington; borough in Clinton Township, Essex County .... Staten Island.

Iselin; village in Woodbridge Township, Middlesex County, on Pennsylvania R. R...................................... Plainfield.

Island; beach on coast of Galloway Township, Atlantic County.. Atlantic City.

Island Beach; village on coast of Galloway Township, Atlantic County.. Atlantic City.

Island Beach; island in Sandy Hook Bay, in Middletown Township, Monmouth County............................. Sandy Hook.

Island Beach; life-saving station on Island Beach in Berkeley Township, Ocean County.............................. Barnegat.

Island Heights; village in Dover Township, Ocean County, on Toms River .... Barnegat.

Island View; village in Woodbridge Township, Middlesex County, on Arthur Kill and on New York and Long Branch R. R... Staten Island.

Isveland Thorofare; passage in coast swamp in Bass River Township, Burlington County............. .... Little Egg Harbor.

Ivanhoe; brook in Millstone and Upper Freehold townships, Monmouth County; flows into Lahaway Creek........... Cassville.

Ives Branch; brook in Bass River township, Burlington County; flows into Wading River...................... Little Egg Harbor.

Names of sheets.

Jack Run; brook in Pemberton and New Hanover townships, Burlington County; flows into North Branch of Rancocas Creek. — Bordentown. Pemberton.

Jackson; township in Ocean County; area 98 square miles.. Cassville.

Jackson; village in Waterford Township, Camden County.. Mount Holly.

Jackson; brook in Randolph Township, Morris County, tributary to Rockaway River .... Lake Hopatcong

Jackson Mills; village in Jackson Township, Ocean County. Cassville.

Jacksonburg; village in Blairstown Township, Warren County, on Jacksonburg Creek........................... Hackettstown.

Jacksonburg; creek rising in Stillwater Township, Sussex County; flows southwest into Warren County, passing through Hardwick Township into Paulins Kill, in east central part of Blairstown Township. — Wallpack. Hackettstown.

Jacksonville; village in Springfield Township, Burlington County .... Burlington.

Jacksonvi'le; village in Madison Township, Middlesex County New Brunswick.

Jacob; creek in Hopewell Township, Mercer County, tributary to Delaware River .... Lambertville.

Jacob; creek in Greenwich Township, Cumberland County, flows into Delaware River.............................. Bayside. ·

Jacobstown; village in New Hanover Township, Burlington County .... Bordentown.

Jake Branch; brook in Berkeley Township, Ocean County, flows into Toms River. — Whitings. Barnegat.

James Branch; brook in Weymouth Township, Atlantic County; flows into Stephen Creek........................ Tuckahoe.

Jamesburg; borough in Monroe township, Middlesex County, at junction of two branches of the Pennsylvania R. R., the Freehold and Jamesburg R. R. and the Camden and Amboy R. R... New Brunswick.

Janvier; village in Franklin Township, Gloucester County... Glassboro.

Jarvis; sound in Lower Township, Cape May County........ Cape May.

Jeffer; creek in Egg Harbor Township, Atlantic County..... Great Egg Harbor.

Jefferson; township in Morris County, area 44 square miles. — Franklin. Greenwood Lake. Hopatcong.

Jefferson; village in Harrison Township, Gloucester County. Philadelphia.

Jeffries; landing in Egg Harbor Township, Atlantic County, on Great Egg Harbor River .... Great Egg Harbor.

Jenkins; channel in Middle Township, Cape May County, connecting Dead Thorofare with Jenkins Sound......... Dennisville.

Jenkins; sound in Middle township, Cape May County...... Dennisville.

Jenkins Neck; high land in Randolph Township, Burlington County .... Mullica.

Jennings; creek in West Milford Township, Passaic County, tributary to Wanaque River .... Greenwood Lake.

Jennings Mill; village in Evesham Township, Burlington County .... Mount Holly.

Jenny; creek in coast swamp in Little Egg Harbor Township, Burlington County .... Little Egg Harbor.

Jenny Jump; mountain in Oxford Township, Warren County; altitude, 1,074 feet. — Delaware Water Gap. Hackettstown.

Jericho; village in Stow Creek Township, Cumberland County, on Horse Run .... Bayside.

Names of sheets.

Jersey City; in Hudson County, on Hudson River, opposite { Staten Island. New York; area, 19 square miles. { Paterson.

Jerseyville; village in Howell Township, Monmouth County. Asbury Park.

Jessie; creek in Little Egg Harbor Township, Burlington County .... Little Egg Harbor.

Jessie; point projecting from Little Egg Harbor Township, Burlington County, into Little Egg Harbor.............. Little Egg Harbor.

Job; creek in Bass River Township, Burlington County; flows into Bass River .... Little Egg Harbor.

Job; creek in Upper Township, Cape May County; flows into Tuckahoe River.. Great Egg Harbor.

Job; point projecting from Egg Harbor Township, Atlantic County, into Great Egg Harbor .... Great Egg Harbor.

Jobstown; village in Springfield Township, Burlington County, on Kinkora Branch, Amboy Division, Pennsylvania R. R.. Bordentown.

Jobstown Bog; marsh in Medford Township, Burlington County .... Mount Holly.

Johney Sledge; island in Little Egg Harbor, in Little Egg Harbor Township, Burlington County .... Little Egg Harbor.

Johnson Place; village in Woodland Township, Burlington County .... Pemberton.

Johnsonburg; village in Frelinghuysen Township, Warren County .... Hackettstown.

Johnsontown; village in Galloway Township, Atlantic County .... Little Egg Harbor.

Jonadab; creek in Dennis Township, Cape May County, flowing into Kill Thorofare..................................... Sea Isle.

Jonas; island in coast swamp in Egg Harbor Township, Atlantic County... Great Egg Harbor.

Jones; island in coast swamp in Lawrence Township, Cumberland County... Bridgeton.

Jones Mill; village in Woodland Township, Burlington County .... Pemberton.

Jordantown; village in Stockton Township, Camden County. Philadelphia.

Juliustown; village in Springfield Township, Burlington County, on Kinkora Branch, Amboy Division, Pennsylvania R. R... Bordentown.

Junction; village in Bethlehem township, Hunterdon County, on Musconetcong River and at junction of New Jersey Central with Delaware, Lackawanna and Western R. R. .... High Bridge.

Kaighn; point of land projecting from Camden City into Delaware River... Philadelphia.

Kalarama; village in Blairstown Township, Warren County, on Paulins Kill and on New York, Susquehanna and Western R. R.. Hackettstown.

Kanouse; mountain range in West Milford Township, Passaic County .... Greenwood Lake.

Karrville; village in Mansfield Township, Warren County, on Pahatcong Creek... Hackettstown.

Keansburg; village in Raritan Township, Monmouth County, on Waycake Creek....................................... Sandy Hook.

Kearney; township in Hudson County; area, 10 square miles. { Paterson. { Staten Island.

Names of sheets.

Kearney; village in Kearney Township, Hudson County, on Passaic River and on Orange Branch of New York and Greenwood Lake R. R................................. Paterson.

Keasbey; creek in Mannington Township, Salem County, flows into Fenwick Creek................................. Salem.

Kelly; point projecting from Lower Penns Neck Township, Salem County, into Delaware River...................... Wilmington.

Kennedy; village in Pohatcong Township, Warren County, on Pohatcong Creek, on New Jersey Central R. R. and on Lehigh Valley R. R.. Easton.

Kenvil; village in Roxbury Township, Morris County, on Morris Canal and on High Bridge Branch of Central R. R. of New Jersey... Lake Hopatcong.

Ker Corners; village in Frelinghuysen Township, Warren County.. Hackettstown.

Kettle; creek rising in Brick Township, forming partial boundary between Brick and Dover townships, Ocean County, flows into Barnegat Bay.......................... Asbury Park.

Kettle Run; brook in Evesham and Medford townships, Burlington County, tributary to Haynes Creek............... Mount Holly.

Kettle Run; brook in Upper Pittsgrove Township, Salem County, flows into Oldman Creek......................... Glassboro.

Key Branch; brook in Winslow Township, Camden County, flows into Great Egg Harbor River....................... Hammonton.

Key East; village in Neptune Township, Monmouth County, on New York and Long Branch R. R..................... Asbury Park.

Keyport; town in Raritan Township, Monmouth County, on Freehold and New York R. R. and on Raritan Bay.... Sandy Hook.

Kinderkamac; village in Washington Township, Bergen County, on New Jersey and New York R. R.............. Paterson.

King; pond in coast swamp in Downe Township, Cumberland County.. Maurice Cove.

King; creek in Linden Township, Union County, tributary to Rahway River... Plainfield.

Kingtown; village in Franklin Township, Hunterdon County, on Cakepoulin Creek .... High Bridge.

Kingwood; township in Hunterdon County; area, 37 square miles. 〔 Easton. Doylestown. Lambertville. High Bridge.

Kingwood; village in Kingwood Township, Hunterdon County, on Lockatong Creek............................... Doylestown.

Kingwood Station; village in Kingwood Township, Hunterdon County, on Delaware River and on Belvidere Division of Pennsylvania R. R .... Doylestown.

Kingsland; village in Union Township, Bergen County, on Boonton Branch of Delaware, Lackawanna and Western R. R.. Paterson.

Kingsland; creek in Union Township, Bergen County, tributary to Hackensack River.............................. Paterson.

Kingston; village in Franklin Township, Somerset County, and South Brunswick Township, Middlesex County, on Millstone River, on Delaware and Raritan Canal, and on Pennsylvania R. R.. Princeton.

Names of sheets.

Kinkora; village in Mansfield Township, Burlington County, on Kinkora Branch, Amboy Division, Pennsylvania R. R. Burlington.

Kirkwood; village in Gloucester Township, Camden County, on Camden and Atlantic R. R...... Philadelphia.

Kitt Thorofare; passage in coast swamp in Dennis Township, Cape May County...... Sea Isle.

Kittatinny; mountain, portion of Appalachian system, extending from Orange County, N. Y., southwest through Sussex and Warren counties, N. J., into Pennsylvania..
{ Bushkill Falls.
Delaware Water Gap.
Wallpack.
Franklin.
Port Jervis.

Klineville; village in Raritan Township, Hunterdon County. High Bridge.

Knowlton; township in Warren County; area, 26 square miles. Delaware Water Gap.

Knowlton; village in Knowlton Township, Warren County. Delaware Water Gap.

Lacey; township in Ocean County; area, 108 square miles.. { Whitings.
Barnegat.

Lacey; village in Lacey Township, Ocean County, on Tuckerton R. R...... Whitings.

Lafayette; township in Sussex County; area, 18 square miles. Franklin.

Lafayette; village in Lafayette Township, Sussex County, on Sussex R. R. and on Paulins Kill River...... Franklin.

Lafayette Mills; village in Marlboro Township, Monmouth County, on Milford Brook...... New Brunswick.

Lahaway; creek in Jackson Township, Ocean County and Upper Freehold Township, Monmouth County, tributary to Crosswick Creek.
{ Bordentown.
Cassville.

Lahaway Plantations; village in Jackson Township, Ocean County...... Cassville.

Lake; bay in coast swamp of Egg Harbor Township, Atlantic County...... Great Egg Harbor.

Lake; creek in Egg Harbor Township, Atlantic County, flows into Great Egg Harbor River...... Great Egg Harbor.

Lake Como: village in Wall Township, Mormouth County, on Lake Como ...... Asbury Park.

Lake Denmark; village in Rockaway Township, Sussex County...... Lake Hopatcong.

Lakedate; village in Winslow Township, Camden County, on Philadelphia and Reading R. R ...... Hammonton.

Lakeside; village in West Milford Township, Passaic County, on western shore of Greenwood Lake...... Greenwood Lake.

Lakewood; town in Brick Township, Ocean County, on Lake Carasaljo...... Asbury Park.

Lambertville; city in Hunterdon County, west of West Amwell Township, on Delaware River and at junction of Flemington Branch with Belvidere Division Pennsylvania R. R...... Lambertville.

Lamington; village in Bedminster Township, Somerset County, on Lamington River...... Somerville.

Lamington; river rising in Morris County, forms boundary ' etween Hunterdon and Somerset counties. and is tributary to North Branch of Raritan River. Its headwaters above boundary of Morris County, are called Black River
{ Lake Hopatcong.
Somerville.

Bull. 118——5

Names of sheets.

Landis; township in Cumberland County; area, 70 square miles.

{ Hammonton.
Bridgeton.
Tuckahoe.
Glassboro.

Landisville; village in Buena Vista Township, Atlantic County, on New Jersey Southern R. R .... Hammonton.

Lanes; pond in Sparta Township, Sussex County .... Franklin.

Lansdowne; village in Franklin Township, Hunterdon County, at junction of Cakepoulin Creek with south Branch of Raritan River, also at junction of Clinton Branch of Lehigh Valley with Lehigh Valley R. R ...... High Bridge.

Larison Corner; village in southern part of Raritan Township, Hunterdon County, on Flemington Branch, Belvidere Division, Pennsylvania R. R .... Lambertville.

Laurel; village in Gloucester Township, Camden County, on Philadelphia and Reading R. R .... Philadelphia.

Laurel; pond in Vernon Township, Sussex County .... Greenwood Lake.

Laurel Mills; village in Gloucester Township, Camden County, on North Branch of Timber Creek .... Philadelphia.

Lavallette; borough on reef in Dover Township, Ocean County, on Philadelphia and Long Branch R. R .... Barnegat.

Lawnton Station; village in Center Township, Camden County, on Philadelphia and Reading R. R .... Philadelphia.

Lawren Branch; brook in Maurice River Township, Cumberland County, flowing west into Manumuskin River... Tuckahoe.

Lawrence; township in Cumberland County; area, 36 square miles.

{ Bayside.
Bridgeton.

Lawrence; township in Mercer County; area, 22 square miles.

{ Princeton.
Bordentown.
Burlington.
Lambertville.

Lawrence; brook rising in South Brunswick Township, Middlesex County, flows northeast, forming boundary between North Brunswick Township and East Brunswick Township, into Raritan River.

{ Princeton.
New Brunswick.

Lawrence Branch; brook in Maurice River Township, Cumberland County, flows into Tuckahoe River............... Tuckahoe.

Lawrence Station; village in Lawrence Township, Mercer County, on Pennsylvania R. R .... Princeton.

Lawrenceville; village in Lawrence Township, Mercer County .... Princeton.

Layton; village in Sandyston Township, Sussex County, on Little Flat Brook..................................... Wallpack.

Layton; mines situated in eastern part of Vernon Township, Sussex County, on New York boundary................... Greenwood Lake.

Leaming Mills; village in Landis Township, Cumberland County .... Tuckahoe.

Lebanon; township in Hunterdon County; area, 26 square miles.

{ Hackettstown.
High Bridge.

Lebanon; village in Clinton Township, Hunterdon County, on Central R. R. of New Jersey......................... High Bridge.

Lebanon Glass Works; village in Woodland Township, Burlington County..................................... Pemberton.

Ledgewood; village in Roxbury Township, Sussex County.. Lake Hopatcong.

Names of sheets.

Lee; meadows in Hanover Township, Morris County......... Morristown.

Leeds; point projecting into coast swamp in Galloway Township, Atlantic County..................................... Atlantic City.

Leedsville; village in Middletown Township, Monmouth County... Sandy Hook.

Leesburg; town in Maurice River Township, Cumberland County, on West Jersey R. R.............................. Tuckahoe.

Leonards; village in West Deptford Township, Gloucester County, on Delaware River R. R........................... Philadelphia.

Leonia; village in Ridgefield Township, Bergen County, on Northern R. R. of New Jersey............................. Harlem.

Lewistown; village in New Hanover Township, Burlington County, at junction of Pemberton and Hightstown R. R. and Kinkora Branch, Amboy Division, Pennsylvania R. R. Bordentown.

Liberty; island off Jersey City, in New York Upper Bay.... Staten Island.

Liberty Corner; village in Bernard Township, Somerset County, on Harrisons Brook............................. Somerville.

Liberty Park Station; village in Haddon Township, Camden County, on Camden and Atlantic R. R............... Philadelphia.

Libertyville; village in Wantage Township, Sussex County... Franklin.

Lincoln; village in South Harrison Township, Gloucester County... Glassboro.

Lincoln Park; village in Pequannock Township, Morris County, on Morris Canal and on Boonton Branch of Delaware, Lackawanna and Western R. R........................... Morristown.

Linden; borough in Union County, on Pennsylvania R. R ... Plainfield.

Linden; township in Union County; area 14 square miles... { Plainfield. { Staten Island.

Linwood; borough in Egg Harbor Township, Atlantic County, on West Jersey R. R.. Great Egg Harbor.

Linwood; village in Ridgefield township, Bergen County, on Hudson River... Harlem.

Little; creek on boundary between Southampton and Medford townships, Burlington County, flows into Haynes Creek. Mount Holly.

Little; sound in Middle Township, Cape May County....... Dennisville.

Little; island in Little Egg Harbor, in Eagleswood Township, Ocean County....................................... Little Egg Harbor.

Little; bay in coast swamp in Galloway Township, Atlantic County... Atlantic City.

Little; pond in eastern part of Sparta Township, Sussex County... Franklin.

Little; pond in Hampton Township, Sussex County.......... Wallpack.

Little; cove, an arm of Lake Hopatcong indenting the northern coast of Roxbury Township, Morris County.......... Lake Hopatcong.

Little Beach; life-saving station on Island Beach .... Atlantic City.

Little Ease Run; brook in Monroe, Glassboro, Clayton, and Franklin townships, Gloucester County, flows into Maurice River.. Glassboro.

Light Egg; life-saving station at south end Tucker Beach... Atlantic City.

Little Egg; harbor on coast of New Jersey, between New Inlet and Barnegat Bay .... Little Egg Harbor.

Little Egg Harbor; township in Burlington County; area, 75 square miles. { Atlantic City. { Whitings. { Little Egg Harbor.

Names of sheets.

Little Egg Harbor; light-house on Tucker Island, in Little Egg Harbor Township, Burlington County............... Little Egg Harbor.

Little Falls; township in Passaic County; area, 6 square miles .... Paterson.

Little Falls; village in Little Falls Township, Passaic County, on Morris Canal, on Passaic River, and on New York and Greenwood Lake R. R....................................... Paterson.

Little Ferry; town in Lodi Township, Bergen County, on Hackensack River .... Paterson.

Little Flat; brook in Sandyston Township, Sussex County, western tributary to Flat Brook .... Wallpack.

Little Hauken; brook in Randolph Township, Burlington { Pemberton.
County, flows into West Branch of Wading River.   { Mullica.

Little Lebanon; creek in Washington Township, Gloucester { Philadelphia.
County, tributary to South Branch of Timber Creek.   { Glassboro.

Little Meadow Run; brook in Egg Harbor Township, Atlantic County, tributary to Patcong Creek .... Great Egg Harbor.

Little Mud Thorofare; passage in coast swamp in Galloway Township, Atlantic County .... Atlantic City.

Little Pond; creek in Downe Township, Cumberland County, flows into Nantuxent Creek............................... Bridgeton.

Little Sandy; island in Barnegat Bay, in Union Township, Ocean County .... Long Beach.

Little Scotch Bonnet; stream in Middle Township, Cape May County, connecting Mulford Creek with Nicholas Channel .... Dennisville.

Little Sheepshead; creek in coast swamp, in Little Egg Harbor Township, Burlington County....................... Little Egg Harbor.

Little Silver; lake in Brick Township, Ocean County....... Asbury Park.

Little Silver; creek in Shrewsbury Township, Monmouth County, flows into Shrewsbury River .... Sandy Hook.

Little Silver; village in Shrewsbury Township, Monmouth County... Sandy Hook.

Little Snake; hill in North Bergen Township, Hudson County; altitude, 23 feet .... Paterson.

Little Thorofare; passage in coast swamp in Little Egg Harbor Township, Burlington County .... Little Egg Harbor.

Little Timber; creek in Logan Township, Gloucester County, flows into Delaware River .... Chester.

Little Timber; creek in Center Township, Camden County, tributary to Big Timber Creek........................... Philadelphia.

Little York; village in Alexandria Township, Hunterdon County .... Easton.

Little York; village in Oxford Township, Warren County .. Delaware Water Gap.

Littleton; village in Hanover Township, Morris County..... Morristown.

Littletown; village in Franklin Township, Hunterdon County .... High Bridge.

Livingston; township in Essex County; area, 17 square miles. Morristown.

Livingston; village in Livingston Township, Essex County . Morristown.

Llewellyn Park; village in West Orange Township, Essex County .... Paterson.

Lockatong; creek rising in Franklin Township, flows (Doylestown.
through Kingwood Township into Delaware River in { Easton.
Delaware Township, Hunterdon County.   (High Bridge.

Names of sheets.

Lockport; village in Raritan Township, Monmouth County, on Chinagarora Creek.. Sandy Hook.

Locktown; village in Delaware Township, Hunterdon County... Lambertville.

Locust; hill in Manalapan Township, Monmouth County; elevation, 263 feet .... New Brunswick.

Locust Corner; village in East Windsor Township, Mercer County... Princeton.

Locust Grove; village in Delaware Township, Camden County... Mount Holly.

Locust Grove; village in Westfield Township, Union County. Plainfield.

Lodi; Township in Bergen County; area, 15 square miles.... Paterson.

Lodi; village in Delaware Township, Camden County....... Mount Holly.

Lodi; town in Lodi Township, Bergen County, on Saddle River and on Lodi branch of New Jersey and New York R. R .... Paterson.

Log Swamp Branch; brook rising in Little Egg Harbor Township, Burlington County, flows northeast into Westecunk Creek in Eagleswood Township, Ocean County...... Little Egg Harbor.

Logan; township in Gloucester County, area 28 square miles. Salem.

London Branch; brook tributary to Repaupo Creek in Greenwich Township, Gloucester County....................... Chester.

Long; meadow in Caldwell Township, Essex County......... Morristown.

Long; point projecting from Dover Township, Ocean County, into Toms River.. Barnegat.

Long; point projecting from Eagleswood Township, Ocean County, into Little Egg Harbor .... Little Egg Harbor.

Long; pond in Andover Township, Sussex County........... Franklin.

Long; pond in Frankford Township, Sussex County......... Wallpack.

Long; pond in Wallpack Township, Sussex County.......... Wallpack.

Long Beach; life-saving station on coast of Eagleswood Township, Ocean County....................................... Long Beach.

Long Branch; life-saving station on coast of Ocean Township, Monmouth County... Sandy Hook.

Long Branch; town in Ocean Township, Monmouth County, on the Atlantic Ocean, on New Jersey Southern R. R. and on New York and Long Branch R. R...................... Sandy Hook.

Long Branch; brook in Ocean and Lacey townships, Ocean County, tributary to North Branch of Forked River..... Whitings.

Long Branch; brook in Jackson Township, Ocean County, flows into Toms River .... Cassville.

Long Branch; brook in Eatontown and Ocean townships, Monmouth County, tributary to Pleasure Bay........... Sandy Hook.

Long Branch Run; brook in Stow Creek Township, Cumberland County, flows into Horse Run....................... Bayside.

Long Cape Island; creek in Lower Township, Cape May County .... Cape May.

Long Causeway; village in Woodland Township, Burlington County.. Whitings.

Long Causeway Branch; brook in Brick Township, Ocean County.. Asbury Park.

Long Cripple; brook in Woodland Township, Burlington County, tributary to Shoal Branch....................... Whitings.

Long Hill; village in Passaic Township, Morris County...... Plainfield.

Names of sheets.

Long Hill; mountain range extending along southern bound- ⎰ Plainfield.
ary of Morris County. Its greatest elevation is 489 feet. ⎱ Somerville.

Long Reach; village in Commercial Township, Cumberland
County, on Maurice River................................ Maurice Cove.

Long Reach; passage in coast swamp in Middle Township, ⎰ Dennisville.
Cape May County. ⎱ Sea Isle.

Long Spring; brook in Woodland Township, Burlington ⎰ Whitings.
County; flows into Governors Mill Brook. ⎱ Pemberton.

Longport; village on coast of Egg Harbor Township, Atlantic County...................................... Great Egg Harbor.

Loper Run; brook in Deerfield Township, Cumberland ⎰ Bridgeton.
County; flows into Cohansey Creek. ⎱ Bayside.

Lopatcong; township in Warren County; area, 9 square
miles .... Easton.

Lopatcong; creek rising in Harmony Township, flows southwest into Delaware River in Lopatcong Township, Warren County... Easton.

Lopatcong; village in Lopatcong Township, Warren County,
on Lopatcong Creek, on Morris Canal, on New Jersey Central R. R. and on Lehigh Valley R. R................. Easton.

Lorillard; village in Raritan Township, Monmouth County.. Sandy Hook.

Losee; pond in Hardiston Township, Sussex County........ Franklin.

Lovelady; island in Barnegat Bay in Union Township, Ocean
County .... Long Beach.

Lovelady Islands; life-saving station on coast of Union
Township, Ocean County.............................. Long Beach.

Low Moor; village on reef in Shrewsbury Township, Monmouth County, on New York and Long Branch R. R...... Sandy Hook.

Low Water Thorofare; passage in coast swamp in Galloway
Township, Atlantic County........................... Atlantic City.

Lower; township in Cape May County; area, 36 square miles ⎰ Dennisville.
⎱ Cape May.

Lower; valley in Lebanon Township, Hunterdon County... High Bridge.

Lower Alloways Creek; township in Salem County; area, ⎰ Bayside.
46 square miles. ⎱ Salem.

Lower Bank; village in Randolph Township, Burlington
County, on Mullica River............................ Mullica.

Lower Chatham Bridge; village in Millburn Township, Essex
County, on Passaic River .... Morristown.

Lower Harmony; village in Harmony Township, Warren
County, on Lopatcong Creek......................... Easton.

Lower Longwood; pond in Jefferson Township, Morris
County .... Lake Hopatcong.

Lower Mill; village in Pemberton Township, Burlington
County .... Pemberton.

Lower Penns Neck; township in Salem County; area, 24
square miles .... Salem.

Lows Hollow; village in Lopatcong Township, Warren
County .... Easton.

Lubbers Run; river rising in Sparta Township, Sussex
County, flows southwest into Musconetcong River, in ⎰ Franklin.
Byram Township, Sussex County. ⎱ Lake Hopatcong.

Lucas Branch; brook in Mullica Township, Atlantic
County, flows in Mullica River...................... Mullica.

Names of sheets.

Ludlam; beach along coast of Upper and Dennis townships, Cape May County.......... Sea Isle.

Ludlam; bay on boundary between Dennis and Upper townships, Cape May County.......... Sea Isle.

Ludlam; creek in Upper Township, Cape May County, tributary to Hughes Creek.......... Great Egg Harbor.

Ludlam Beach; light on Ludlam Beach.......... Sea Isle.

Ludlam Thorofare; passage in coast swamp in Dennis Township, Cape May County.......... Sea Isle.

Lumberton; township in Burlington County; area, 21 square miles.......... Mount Holly.

Lumberton; village in Lumberton Township, Burlington County, on Philadelphia, Marlton and Medford R. R..... Mount Holly.

Lummistown; village in Lawrence Township, Cumberland County, on Cedar Creek.......... Bridgeton

Lupatcong; creek in Matawan and Raritan townships, Monmouth County, flows into Raritan Bay.......... Sandy Hook.

Lyons; village in Bernard Township, Somerset County, on Passaic and Delaware Branch of Delaware, Lackawanna and Western R. R.......... Somerville.

Lyons Farms; village in Union Township, Union County ... Staten Island.

Lyonsville; village in Rockaway Township, Morris County.. Morristown.

Lyndhurst; village in Union Township, Bergen County, on Passaic River and on Boonton Branch of Delaware, Lackawanna and Western R. R.......... Paterson.

Macannippuck; creek in Stow Creek Township, Cumberland County, tributary to Newport Creek.......... Bayside.

Macopin; lake in West Milford Township, Passaic County.. Greenwood Lake.

Macopin; village in West Milford Township, Passaic County. Greenwood Lake.

Mad Horse; creek in Lower Alloways Creek Township, Salem County, flows into Delaware River.......... Bayside.

Madison; township in Middlesex County; area, 37 square miles. { New Brunswick. { Sandy Hook.

Madison; borough in Chatham Township, Morris County, on Delaware, Lackawanna and Western R. R.......... Morristown.

Magnolia; village in Oldman Township, Salem County, on Delaware River R. R.......... Chester.

Magnolia; village in Pemberton Township, Burlington County.......... Pemberton.

Magnolia Station; village in Center Township, Camden County, on Philadelphia and Reading R. R.......... Philadelphia.

Mahoras; brook in Middletown and Holmdel townships, Monmouth County, tributary to Waycake Creek.......... Sandy Hook.

Mahwah; village in Hohokus Township, Bergen County, on New York, Lake Erie and Western R. R.......... Ramapo.

Main; point projecting from Stafford Township, Ocean County, into Manahawken Bay.......... Long Beach.

Main; channel in coast swamp in Galloway Township, Atlantic County, opens into Absecon Inlet.......... Atlantic City.

Main; channel in coast swamp connecting Ludlam Bay with Corson Inlet, in Upper Township, Cape May County..... Sea Isle.

Main; channel in Dennis and Middle townships, Cape May County, connecting Townsend Sound with Townsend Inlet.......... Sea Isle.

Names of sheets.

Main Marsh Thorofare; passage in coast swamp in Galloway Township, Atlantic County........................... Atlantic City.

Maine Avenue; station on New Jersey Southern R. R., in Landis Township, Cumberland County.................... Hammonton.

Major Run; brook on boundary between Pilesgrove and Mannington townships, Salem County, flows into Salem Creek .... Salem.

Malaga; village in Franklin Township, Gloucester County.. Glassboro.

Malapardis; village in Hanover Township, Morris County.. Morristown.

Manahawken; bay in Stafford and Union townships, Ocean County .... Long Beach.

Manahawken; creek in Stafford Township, Ocean County, flows into Manahawken Bay .... Long Beach.

Manahawken; village in Stafford Township, Ocean County, on Tuckerton R. R................................... Little Egg Harbor.

Manalapan; township in Monmouth County; area, 31 square miles. { Cassville. / New Brunswick.

Manalapan; brook tributary to South River, in Manalapan Township, Monmouth County, and Monroe Township, Middlesex County .... New Brunswick.

Manalapan; village in Manalapan Township, Monmouth County .... New Brunswick.

Manantico; village in Millville Township, Cumberland County .... Bridgeton.

Manantico; creek in Buena Vista Township, Atlantic County, Landis and Millville townships, Cumberland County, flows into Maurice River. It forms a partial boundary between Millville and Commercial townships, Cumberland County. } Tuckahoe. / Bridgeton.

Manapaqua Branch; brook in Manchester Township, Ocean County, flows into Union Branch of Toms River......... Cassville.

Manasquan; river rising in Freehold township, flows southeast through Howell and Wall townships, and forming partial boundary between Wall and Brick townships, Monmouth County, empties into Manasquan Inlet. } Cassville. / Asbury Park.

Manasquan; inlet, at mouth of Manasquan River, extending from Atlantic Ocean between Brick Township, Ocean County, and Wall Township, Monmouth County......... Asbury Park.

Manasquan; town in Wall Township, Monmouth County, on Philadelphia and Long Branch R. R..................... Asbury Park.

Manchester; township in Passaic County; area, 11 square miles .... Paterson.

Manchester; township in Ocean County; area, 83 square miles. { Whitings. / Cassville.

Manchester; town in Manchester Township, Ocean County, at junction of New Jersey Southern and Philadelphia and Long Branch railroads.............................. Cassville.

Mannington; township in Salem County; area, 38 square miles .... Salem.

Mannington; creek in Mannington Township, Salem County, tributary to Salem Creek .... Salem.

Mansfield; township in Warren County; area, 30 square miles .... Hackettstown.

Mansfield; township in Burlington County; area, 23 square miles. { Bordentown. / Burlington.

Names of sheets.

Mansfield; village in Mansfield Township, Burlington County .... Bordentown.

Mansfield Square; village in Bordentown Township, Burlington County .... Bordentown.

Mantoloking; life-saving station on reef in Brick Township, Ocean County .... Asbury Park.

Mantoloking; village on reef in Brick Township, Ocean County, on Philadelphia and Long Branch R. R. .... Asbury Park.

Mantua; creek rising in Glassboro Township, flows northwest through Gloucester County into Delaware River at Greenwich Township. } Philadelphia. Glassboro.

Mantua; township in Gloucester County; area, 19 square miles .... { Philadelphia. Glassboro.

Mantua; village in Mantua Township, Gloucester County, on Mantua Creek .... Philadelphia.

Manumuskin; river heading in Buena Vista Township, Atlantic County, flows southwest, forming boundary between Maurice River Township, on the east, and Landis, Millville, and Commercial townships on the west, into Maurice River .... Tuckahoe.

Manumuskin; village in Maurice River Township, Cumberland County, on Manumuskin River .... Tuckahoe.

Manunkachunk; village in Oxford Township, Warren County, on Delaware River, on Delaware, Lackawanna and Western R. R., and at its junction with the Belvidere Division of Pennsylvania R. R. .... Delaware Water Gap.

Maple Grange; village in Vernon Township, Sussex County, on Lehigh and Hudson River R. R. .... Greenwood Lake.

Maple Island; creek in Newark City, Essex County, tributary to Newark Bay .... Staten Island.

Maple Root Branch; brook in Jackson Township, Ocean County, flows into Toms River .... Cassville.

Maple Run; brook in Egg Harbor Township, Atlantic County, flows into Patcong Creek .... Great Egg Harbor.

Maple Shade Station; village in Chester Township, Burlington County, on Pennsylvania R. R., Amboy Division..... Philadelphia.

Maplewood; village in South Orange Township, Essex County, on Delaware, Lackawanna and Western R. R., and on East Branch of Rahway River...................... Plainfield.

Marble; mountain in Lopatcong and Harmony townships, Warren County .... Easton.

Marcia; lake in Montague Township, Sussex County .... Port Jervis.

Mare Run; brook in Hamilton Township, Atlantic County, flows into Great Egg Harbor River. { Tuckahoe. Great Egg Harbor.

Marion; part of Jersey City, on Hackensack River........... Staten Island.

Marksboro; village in Hardwick Township, Warren County, on Paulins Kill and on New York, Susquehanna and Western R. R .... Hackettstown.

Marlboro; township in Monmouth County; area, 31 square miles. { Sandy Hook. New Brunswick.

Marlboro; village in Marlboro Township, Monmouth County, on Freehold and New York R. R. .... Sandy Hook.

Marlton; village in Evesham Township, Burlington County on Philadelphia, Marlton and Medford R. R. .... Mount Holly.

Names of sheets.

Marquis; creek in Matawan Township, Monmouth County, flowing into Raritan Bay..................................... Sandy Hook.

Marsh Elder; group of islands in Little Egg Harbor, Eagleswood Township, Ocean County............................ Long Beach.

Marsh Elder; channel in coast marsh, in Little Egg Harbor Township, Burlington County............................ Little Egg Harbor.

Marsh Elder; island in Barnegat Bay, in Union Township, Ocean County...................................... Long Beach.

Marshall; island off coast of Kingwood Township, Hunterdon County, in Delaware River................................ Doylestown.

Marshall Corner; village in Hopewell Township, Mercer County... Lambertville.

Marshalltown; village in Mannington Township, Salem County.. Salem.

Marshalville; village in Upper Township, Cape May County, on branch of Tuckahoe River............................ Tuckahoe.

Martha; village in Bass River Township, Burlington County, on Oswego River or East Branch of Wading River....... Mullica.

Martins Creek Station; village in Harmony Township, Warren County, on Delaware River and at junction of Belvidere Division and Martins Creek Branch Pennsylvania R. R. } Delaware Water Gap.

Martinsville; village in Bridgewater Township, Somerset County... Somerville.

Mary Ann Furnace; village in Pemberton Township, Burlington County .... Pemberton.

Mashipacong; pond in Montague Township, Sussex County. Port Jervis.

Mashipacong; island off Montague Township, Sussex County, in Delaware River. { Port Jervis. / Milford.

Maskell Mill; village in Lower Alloways Creek Township, Salem County .... Bayside.

Mason; creek on boundary between Lumberton and Mount Laurel townships, Burlington County, flows into South Branch of Rancocas Creek .... Mount Holly.

Masonicus; village in Hohokus Township, Bergen County.. Ramapo.

Masonville; village in Mount Laurel Township, Burlington County, on Pennsylvania R. R........................... Mount Holly.

Mat Gut; brook in Middle Township, Cape May County, flowing into Dung Thorofare............................... Dennisville.

Matawan; township in Monmouth County; area, 8 square miles. { Sandy Hook. / New Brunswick.

Matawan; borough in Matawan Township, Monmouth County, on Matawan Creek............................... Sandy Hook.

Matawan; creek in Matawan Township, Monmouth County, flowing into Raritan Bay............................... Sandy Hook.

Matchaponix; village in Monroe Township, Middlesex County, on Matchaponix River........................... New Brunswick.

Mathew; brook in West Deptford Township, Gloucester County, tributary to Woodbury Creek .... Philadelphia.

Matthew; brook in Egg Harbor Township, Atlantic County, flows into Great Egg Harbor River...................... Great Egg Harbor.

Maurice; river in Gloucester County; flows into Maurice River Cove. { Glassboro. / Bridgeton. / Tuckahoe. / Maurice Cove.

Names of sheets.

Maurice River; township in Cumberland County; area, 105 square miles.
{ Bridgeton. Maurice Cove. Tuckahoe. Dennisville. }

Maurice River; light-house on coast of Maurice River Township, Cumberland County .... Maurice Cove.

Maurice River; cove projecting from Delaware Bay into Downe and Commercial Townships, Cumberland County. Maurice Cove.

Maurice River Neck; peninsula extending into swamp in Maurice River Township, Cumberland County .... Maurice Cove.

Mauricetown; station in Commercial township, Cumberland County, on Central R. R. of New Jersey .... Bridgeton.

Mauricetown; village in Maurice River Township, Cumberland County, on Maurice River .... Tuckahoe.

May Landing; town in Hamilton Township, Atlantic County, on Great Egg Harbor River .... Great Egg Harbor.

Mayetta; village in Stafford Township, Ocean County, on Tuckerton R. R.. Little Egg Harbor.

Mayville; village in Middle Township, Cape May County... Dennisville.

Maywood; village in Midland Township, Bergen County... Paterson.

McAfee; village in Vernon Township, Sussex County, on Lehigh and Hudson River R. R............................ Franklin.

McClellan; village, part of Orange City, Essex County, on Orange Branch of New York and Greenwood Lake R. R.. Paterson.

McDonald Branch; brook in Woodland Township, Burlington County, tributary to Mount Misery Brook .... Pemberton.

McGellaird; brook in Freehold and Manalapan townships, Monmouth County, flowing into Wemrock Brook .... New Brunswick.

McKeetown; village in Hamilton Township, Atlantic County .... Great Egg Harbor.

Meadows; village in Kearney Township, Hudson County, at junction of Pennsylvania R. R. and Delaware, Lackawanna and Western R. R.................................. Staten Island.

Mechanicsville; village in Upper Freehold Township, Monmouth County .... Cassville.

Mechanicsville; village in Gloucester Township, Camden County .... Philadelphia.

Mechanicsville; village in Raritan Township, Monmouth County .... Sandy Hook.

Mechesactauxin Branch; brook in Waterford Township, Camden County, and Hammonton and Mullica townships, Atlantic County, flowing into Mullica River.
{ Mount Holly. Mullica. Hammonton. }

Medford; township in Burlington County; area, 42 square miles .... Mount Holly.

Medford; town in Medford Township, Burlington County, on Haynes Creek and Philadelphia, Marlton and Medford R. R.. Mount Holly.

Melrose; village in Evesham Township, Burlington County. Mount Holly.

Mendham; township in Morris County; area, 24 square miles { Lake Hopatcong. Somerville. }

Mendham; village in Mendham Township, Morris County .. Lake Hopatcong.

Menlo Park; village in Raritan Township, Middlesex County, on Pennsylvania R. R................................... Plainfield.

Names of sheets.

Mercer; county in central part of the State; area, 228 square miles.
{ Lambertville.
Burlington.
Princeton.
Bordentown.
Cassville.
New Brunswick.

Mercerville; village in Hamilton Township, Mercer County. Bordentown.

Merchantville; borough in Camden County, on Pennsylvania R. R., Amboy Division .... Philadelphia.

Meriden; village in Rockaway Township, Morris County, on Beaver Brook.. Morristown.

Merrygold Branch; brook in Bass River Township, Burlington County, flowing into Wading River.............. Little Egg Harbor.

Metedeconk; river rising in Freehold Township, Monmouth County, flows southeast across Monmouth and Ocean counties into Barnegat Bay.
{ Cassville.
Asbury Park.

Metedeconk Neck; point of land between Metedeconk River and Kettle Creek in Brick Township, Ocean County...... Asbury Park.

Metuchen; town in Raritan Township, Middlesex County, where the Lehigh Valley and the Pennsylvania R. R. cross each other..................................... Plainfield.

Michaels Run; brook in Manchester Township, Ocean County, tributary to Wrangel Brook........................... Whitings.

Mickleton; village in East Greenwich Township, Gloucester County, on West Jersey R. R..................... Philadelphia.

Middle; township in Cape May County; area, 93 square miles.
{ Dennisville.
Sea Isle.

Middle; river in swamp in Weymouth Township, Atlantic County, flowing into Great Egg Harbor River.
{ Great Egg Harbor.
Tuckahoe.

Middle; brook in Bedminster Township, Somerset County, tributary to North Branch of Raritan River............. Somerville.

Middle; brook in Somerset County, tributary to Raritan River...................................... Somerville.

Middle Branch; brook in Maurice River Township, Cumberland County, tributary to Muskee Creek............... Tuckahoe.

Middle Channel; passage in coast swamp in Middle and Dennis townships, Cape May County..................... Sea Isle.

Middle Forge; village in Rockaway Township, Morris County, on Morris County R R...................... Lake Hopatcong.

Middle Marsh; creek in Fairfield Township, Cumberland County, flowing into Delaware River.................... Bayside.

Middle Run; brook in Lawrence Township, Cumberland County, flowing into Nantuxent Creek................... Bridgeton.

Middle Thorofare; passage in coast swamp in Galloway Township, Atlantic County........................... Atlantic City.

Middle Thorofare; passage in coast swamp in Upper Township, Cape May County .... Sea Isle.

Middle Valley; village in Washington Township, Morris County, on South Branch of Raritan River and on New Jersey Central R. R....................... Hackettstown.

Middlebush; village in Franklin Township, Somerset County, on Millstone Branch of Pennsylvania R. R.............. Princeton.

Middlebush; brook in Franklin Township, Somerset County, tributary to Six Mile Run..................... Princeton.

Names of sheets.

Middlesex; county in central part of the State; area, 324 square miles.
- Somerville.
- Princeton.
- Plainfield.
- New Brunswick.
- Sandy Hook.
- Staten Island.

Middletown; township in Monmouth County; area, 43 square miles .... Sandy Hook.

Middletown; village in Upper Township, Cape May County. Great Egg Harbor.

Middletown; village in Middletown Township, Monmouth County, on New York and Long Branch R. R............. Sandy Hook.

Middleville; village in Stillwater Township, Sussex County, on Trout Brook....................................... Wallpack.

Midland; township in Bergen County; area, 16 square miles. Paterson.

Midland Park; village in Franklin and Ridgewood townships, Bergen County, on New York, Susquehanna and Western R. R.. Paterson.

Midvale; village in Pompton Township, Passaic County, on Wanaque River and on New York and Greenwood Lake R. R.. Greenwood Lake.

Midvale; village in Union Township, Hunterdon County, on Lehigh Valley R. R .... High Bridge,

Midwood; village in Jackson Township, Ocean County.... Cassville.

Mile; run, forming western boundary of New Brunswick City and tributary to Raritan River.
- New Brunswick.
- Plainfield.

Mile; run in Shamong and Randolph townships, Burlington County, flowing into West Branch of Wading River..... Pemberton.

Mile Thorofare; passage in coast swamp in Galloway Township, Atlantic County..................................... Atlantic City.

Milford; brook in Marlboro and Manalapan townships, Monmouth County, flowing into McGellaird Brook .... New Brunswick.

Milford; village in East Windsor Township, Mercer County, on Millstone River.................................... Princeton.

Milford; village in Waterford Township, Camden County, and Evesham Township, Burlington County............. Mount Holly.

Milford; village in Holland Township, Hunterdon County, on Delaware River and on Pennsylvania R. R., Belvidere Division .... Easton.

Mill; brook in Randolph Township, Morris County, tributary to Rockaway River .... Lake Hoptacong.

Mill; brook in Montague Township, Sussex County, flowing into Delaware River .... Port Jervis.

Mill; creek in Dennis Township, Cape May County.......... Sea Isle.

Mill; creek in Egg Harbor Township, Atlantic County, tributary to Patcong Creek................................. Great Egg Harbor.

Mill; creek in Fairfield Township, Cumberland County, flowing into Cohansey Creek................................. Bridgeton.

Mill; creek heading in Deerfield Township, forms partial boundary between it and Bridgeton Township, flows through portion of Millville Township, Cumberland County, into Maurice River .... Bridgeton.

Mill; creek in Lower Township, Cape May County.......... Cape May.

Names of sheets.

Mill; creek in Downe Township, Cumberland County, flowing into Dividing Creek...................................... Bridgeton.

Mill; creek in Greenwich Township, Cumberland County, flowing into Molly Wheaten Run.......................... Bayside.

Mill; creek in Berkeley Township, Ocean County, flowing into Toms River .... Barnegat.

Mill; creek in North Bergen Township, Hudson County, tributary to Hackensack River................................. Paterson.

Mill; creek in Stafford Township, Ocean County, flowing { Little Egg Harbor.
into Little Egg Harbor. { Long Beach.

Mill; creek on boundary between Burlington and Willingboro townships, Burlington County, flowing into Rancocas Creek... Burlington.

Mill Branch; brook in Egg Harbor Township, Atlantic County, tributury to Patcong Creek....................... Great Egg Harbor.

Mill Thorofare; passage in coastsswamp in Dennis Township, Cape May County.. Sea Isle.

Millbrook; village in Pahaquarry Township, Warren County, on Vancampens Brook .... Wallpack.

Millbrook; village in Randolph Township, Morris County, on Mill Brook... Lake Hopatcong.

Millburn; township in Essex County; area, 10 square miles. { Plainfield. { Morristown.

Millburn; village in Millburn Township, Essex County, on Delaware, Lackawanna and Western R. R................. Plainfield.

Miller; creek in Upper Township, Cape May County, flowing into Peck Bay .... Great Egg Harbor.

Millham; village in Hamiliton Township, Mercer County, on Pennsylvania R. R. and on Assanpink Creek............. Bordentown.

Millington; village in Passaic Township, Morris County, on Passaic and Delaware R. R. and on Passaic River ...... Somerville.

Millstone; township in Monmouth County; area, 40 square { Cassville.
miles. { New Brunswick.

Millstone; river rising in Millstone Township, Monmouth ⌠ Somerville.
County, flows northwest, forming boundary between Mer- | Princeton.
cer and Middlesex counties, thence northward through ⟩ New Brunswick.
Somerset County and enters the Raritan River. | Cassville.

Millstone; village in Hillsboro Township, Somerset County, { Somerville.
on Millstone River, opposite East Millstone. { Princeton.

Milltown; borough in North Brunswick Township, Middlesex County, on Lawrence Brook.............................. New Brunswick.

Milltown; village in Kingwood Township, Hunterdon County, on Lockatong Creek .... Doylestown.

Milltown; village in Springfield Township, Union County, on East Branch of Rahway River......................... Plainfield.

Milltown; village in Branchburg Township, Somerset County, on North Branch of Raritan River...................... Somerville.

Millville; township in Cumberland County; area, 46 square { Bridgeton.
miles. { Tuckahoe.

Millville; city in Millville Township, Cumberland County, on Maurice River .... Bridgeton.

Millville; village in Ocean Township, Ocean County........ Whitings.

Milton; village in Vernon Township, Sussex County........ Port Jervis.

Milton; village in Jefferson Township, Morris County ...... Franklin.

A GEOGRAPHIC DICTIONARY OF NEW JERSEY. **79**

Mine; brook in Bernard Township, Somerset County, tributary to North Branch of Raritan River .... Somerville.

Mine Hill; village in Randolph Township, Morris County... Lake Hopatcong.

Minisink; island off coast of Montague and Sandston townships, Sussex County, in Delaware River .... Milford.

Minnisink; village in Jefferson Township, Morris County... Lake Hopatcong.

Miry Run; brook on boundary between Hamilton and Egg Harbor townships, flowing into Great Egg Harbor River. Great Egg Harbor.

Miry Run; brook in Washington and Hamilton townships, Mercer County, tributary to Assanpink Creek .... Bordentown.

Molly Wheaten Run; brook in Greenwich Township, Cumberland County, flowing into Cohansey Creek .... Bayside.

Moonachie; village in Lodi Township, Bergen County...... Paterson.

Moore; creek in Hopewell Township, Mercer County, tributary to Delaware River .... Lambertville.

Moorestown; village in Chester Township, Burlington County, on Pennsylvania R. R .... Mount Holly.

Mooseback; pond in Jefferson Township, Morris County.... Franklin.

Monds; island in Delaware River off coast of Greenwich Township, Gloucester County .... Chester.

Money; islands in Toms River in Dover Township, Ocean County .... Barnegat.

Money; island in swamp in Independence Township, Warren County .... Hackettstown.

Monks; village in Pompton Township, Passaic County, on Wanaque River and on New York and Greenwood Lake R. R.. Greenwood Lake.

Monmouth; county in central part of State; area, 538 square miles.
{ Bordentown.
Cassville.
New Brunswick.
Sandy Hook.
Asbury Park.

Monmouth; park in Eatontown Township, Monmouth County.. Sandy Hook.

Monmouth Beach; life-saving station on reef in Ocean Township, Monmouth County .... Sandy Hook.

Monmouth Beach; village in Ocean Township, Monmouth County, on New York and Long Branch R. R............. Sandy Hook.

Monmouth Junction; village in South Brunswick Township, Middlesex County, on Pennsylvania R. R................. Princeton.

Monongahela; brook in Deptford Township, Gloucester County, tributary to Mantua Creek .... Philadelphia.

Monroe; township in Middlesex County; area, 44 square miles .... New Brunswick.

Monroe; township in Gloucester County; area, 46 square miles. { Hammonton. Glassboro.

Monroe; village in Hanover Township, Morris County...... Morristown.

Monroe Corner; village in Sparta Township, Sussex County, on Sussex R. R.. Franklin.

Monroe Forge; village in Weymouth Township, Atlantic County, on South River................................... Tuckahoe.

Monroeville; village in Franklin Township, Gloucester County .... Glassboro.

Monroeville; village in Franklin Township, Gloucester County, on West Jersey R. R............................... Glassboro.

80   A GEOGRAPHIC DICTIONARY OF NEW JERSEY.

Names of sheets.

Montague; township in Sussex County; area, 45 square miles.
{ Milford. Port Jervis. Franklin. Wallpack. }

Montague; village in Montague Township, Sussex County, on Delaware River .... Milford.

Montana; village in Harmony Township, Warren County... Delaware Water Gap.

Montclair; township in Essex County; area, 6 square miles. Paterson.

Montclair; town in Montclair Township, Essex County, on New York and Greenwood Lake R. R., and on Bloomfield Branch of Delaware, Lackawanna and Western R. R..... Paterson.

Montclair Heights; village in Montclair Township, Essex County, on New York and Greenwood Lake R. R......... Paterson.

Montgomery; township in Somerset county; area, 33 square miles .... Princeton.

Montgomery; village in Hillsboro Township, Somerset County .... Lambertville.

Montvale; village in Washington Township, Bergen County, on New Jersey and New York R. R...................... Ramapo.

Montville; village in Montville Township, Morris County, on Morris Canal, and on Boonton Branch of Delaware, Lackawanna and Western R. R............................... Morris 'wn.

Montville; township in Morris County; area, 19 square miles. Morristown.

Mordecai; island in Little Egg Harbor, in Eagleswood Township, Ocean County...................................... Little Egg Harbor.

Morgan; village in Sayreville Township, Middlesex County. New Brunswick.

Morganville; village in Marlboro Township, Monmouth County, on Freehold and New York R. R................. Sandy Hook.

Morris; township in Morris County; area, 19 square miles.. { Morristown. Lake Hopatcong. }

Morris; county in northern part of State; area, 480 square miles.
{ Greenwood Lake. Franklin. Morristown. Plainfield. Somerville. Lake Hopatcong. Hackettstown. High Bridge. }

Morris; canal connecting Phillipsburg on the Delaware with Hudson River at Jersey City.
{ Easton. Delaware Water Gap. Hackettstown. Lake Hopatcong. Morristown. Paterson. Staten Island. }

Morris; pond in Sparta Township, Sussex County........... Franklin.

Morris County Junction; village in Roxbury Township, Morris County................................... Lake Hopatcong

Morris Plains; village in Hanover Township, Morris County, on Delaware, Lackawanna and Western R. R............. Morristown.

Morris Spring; brook in Randolph Township, Morris County, tributary to Jackson Brook.............................. Lake Hopatcong.

Morris Station; village in Stockton Township, Camden County, on Pensauken River and on Pennsylvania R. R.. Philadelphia.

Names of sheets.

Morristown; village in Madison Township, Middlesex County. New Brunswick.

Morristown; city in Morris Township, Morris County, on Whippany River, and on Delaware, Lackawanna and Western R. R.. Morristown.

Morrisville; village in Stockton Township, Camden County. Philadelphia.

Morrisville; village in Holmdel Township, Monmouth County. Sandy Hook.

Morses; creek in Linden Township, Union County, tributary to Arthur Kill .... Staten Island.

Mosquito; cove projecting from Barnegat Bay into Dover Township, Ocean County................................. Barnegat.

Mounce; creek on boundary between Hopewell and Greenwich townships, Cumberland County, flowing into Cohansey Creek.. Bayside.

Mount; village in Washington Township, Burlington County. Mullica.

Mount Airy; village in West Amwell Township, Hunterdon County.. Lambertville.

Mount Bethel; village in Mansfield Township, Warren County. Hackettstown.

Mount Bethel; village in Warren Township, Somerset County. Somerville.

Mount Ephraim; village in Center Township, Camden County, at terminus of Camden, Gloucester and Mount Ephraim R. R.. Philadelphia.

Mount Fern; hill in Randolph Township, Morris County; altitude, 1,003 feet... Lake Hopatcong.

Mount Freedom; village in Randolph Township, Morris County .... Lake Hopatcong.

Mount Herman; village in Hope Township, Warren County. Hackettstown.

Mount Holly; hill in Northampton Township, Burlington County; elevation, 180 feet............................... Burlington.

Mount Holly; village in Northampton Township, Burlington County, on Rancocas Creek. { Mount Holly. { Burlington.

Mount Hope; village in Rockaway Township, Morris County, on High Bridge Branch of Central R. R. of New Jersey.. Lake Hopatcong.

Mount Horeb; village in Warren Township, Somerset County. Somerville.

Mount Jemima; hill in Washington Township, Burlington County .... Mullica.

Mount Joy; village in Holland Township, Hunterdon County, on Delaware River and on Pennsylvania R. R., Belvidere Division .... Easton.

Mount Laurel; township in Burlington County; area, 22 square miles... Mount Holly.

Mount Laurel; hill in Mount Laurel Township, Burlington County; elevation, 173 feet............................... Mount Holly.

Mount Mills; village in Monroe Township, Middlesex County, on Matchaponix Brook.................................... New Brunswick.

Mount Misery; brook heading in three branches, North, Middle, and South branches, tributary to North Branch of Rancocas Creek, in Manchester Township, Ocean County, and Woodland and Pembertown townships, Burlington County. } Whitings. Pemberton.

Mount Misery; village in Pemberton Township, Burlington County, on Mount Misery Brook.......................... Pemberton.

Mount Olive; township in Morris County; area, 32 square miles. { Hackettstown. { Lake Hopatcong.

Names of sheets.

Mount Olive; village in Mount Olive Township, Morris County, on Turkey Brook............................... Lake Hopatcong.

Mount Pisgah; village in Frankford Township, in Sussex County, on Paulins Kill................................... Wallpack.

Mount Pleasant; hills in Marlboro and Holmdel townships, Monmouth County.. Sandy Hook.

Mount Pleasant; village in Pilesgrove Township, Salem County.. Salem.

Mount Pleasant; village in Matawan Township, Monmouth County, on Freehold and New York R. R................. Sandy Hook.

Mount Pleasant; village in Dennis Township, Cape May County, on West Jersey R. R............................ Dennisville.

Mount Pleasant; village in Egg Harbor Township, Atlantic County... Great Egg Harbor.

Mount Pleasant; village in Alexandria Township, Hunterdon County, on Harihokake Creek .... Easton.

Mount Rose; village in Hopewell Township, Mercer County. Princeton.

Mount Royal; village in East Greenwich Township, Gloucester County, on West Jersey R. R...................... Philadelphia.

Mount Salem; village in Wantage Township, Sussex County. Port Jervis.

Mountain; village in South Orange Township, Essex County, on Delaware, Lackawanna and Western R. R............. Morristown.

Mountain; pond in Roxbury Township, Morris County...... Lake Hopatcong.

Mountain View; village in Wayne Township, Passaic County, on Pompton River, on Morris Canal, and on New York and Greenwood Lake R. R .... Morristown.

Mountainville; village in Tewksbury Township, Hunterdon County, on North Branch of Rockaway Creek........... High Bridge.

Mowers; village in Upper Alloways Creek Township, Salem County, on West Jersey R. R............................. Salem.

Muckshaw; pond in Andover Township, Sussex County.... Wallpack.

Mud; pond in Pompton Township, Passaic County.......... Greenwood Lake.

Mud; pond in Vernon Township, Sussex County............ Franklin.

Mud; pond in Stillwater Township, Sussex County .... Wallpack.

Mud; pond in Hardwick Township, Warren County........ Wallpack.

Mud Thorofare; passage in coast swamp in Galloway Township, Atlantic County....................................... Atlantic City.

Mud Thorofare; passage in coast swamp in Dennis Township, Cape May County..................................... Sea Isle.

Muddy; brook in Hope Township, Warren County, tributary to Honey Run .... Hackettstown.

Muddy; creek in Lower Alloways Creek Township, Salem County, flows into Delaware River....................... Bayside.

Muddy; run in Bedminster Township, Somerset County, tributary to Lamington River............................. Somerville.

Muddy Ford; brook in Howell Township, Monmouth County, flows into Metedeconk River .... Asbury Park.

Muddy Hole; passage in coast swamp in Middle Township, Cape May County.. Dennisville.

Muirheads; village in Raritan Township, Hunterdon County, on Flemington Branch, Belvidere Division, Pennsylvania R. R... Lambertville.

Mulford; creek in Middle Township, Cape May County, flowing into Scotch Bonnet..................................... Dennisville.

Names of sheets.

Mulford Station; village in Andover Township, Sussex County, on Lehigh and Hudson River R. R .... Franklin.

Mulhockaway; creek rising in Bethlehem and Union townships, Hunterdon County, tributary to Spruce Run ...... High Bridge.

Mullica; township in Atlantic County; area, 55 square miles. { Hammonton. Mullica.

Mullica, or Atsion; river rising in Waterford Township, Camden County, flows southeast, forming boundary between Burlington County on the north and Camden and Atlantic counties on the south, into Great Bay. { Mount Holly. Hammonton. Mullica. Little Egg Harbor.

Mullica Hill; village in Harrison Township, Gloucester County .... Glassboro.

Munion Field; village in Bass River Township, Burlington County .... Little Egg Harbor.

Murray Hill; village in New Providence Township, Union County, on Passaic and Delaware R. R.................... Plainfield.

Murrell Branch; brook in Winslow Township, Camden County, flows into Great Egg Harbor River............ .... Hammonton.

Musconetong; mountain ridge extending through western part of Hunterdon County. { Easton. High Bridge.

Musconetong; village in Pohatcong Township, Warren County, at junction of Musconetong River with Delaware River on Pennsylvania R. R., Belvidere Division........ Easton.

Musconetong; valley lying between Warren and Hunterdon counties............................ .... Easton.

Musconetong; river draining Lake Hopatcong in Sussex County, flows southwest, forming boundary between Morris, Sussex, Hunterdon, and Warren counties, into Delaware River at southwest extremity of Warren County. { Lake Hopatcong. Hackettstown. High Bridge. Easton.

Muskee; creek rising in Maurice River Township, Cumberland County, flowing into Maurice River................. Tuckahoe.

Muskingum; brook in Shamong Township, Burlington County, tributary to Springer Creek...................... Pemberton.

Musquapsink; creek in Washington Township, Bergen County, tributary to Pascock Creek..................... Paterson.

Myrtle; village in Hampton Township, Sussex County...... Wallpack.

Nacote; creek in Galloway Township, Atlantic County, flowing into Mullica River. { Mullica. Little Egg Harbor. Great Egg Harbor.

Nantuxent; creek in boundary between Downe and Lawrence townships, Cumberland County, flowing into Delaware River .... Bridgeton.

Nantuxent; point on coast of Downe Township, Cumberland County .... Bridgeton.

Naughright; village in Washington Township, Morris County, on South Branch of Raritan River .... Lake Hopatcong

Navesink; village in Middeltown Township, Monmouth County .... Sandy Hook.

Navesink; river on boundary between Middletown and Shrewsbury townships, Monmouth County, flowing into Sandy Hook Bay... Sandy Hook.

Navesink; lights on Highlands of Navesink .... Sandy Hook.

Navesink Avenue; village in Middletown Township, Monmouth County .... Sandy Hook.

Names of sheets.

Navesink Beach; village on reef in Middletown Township, Monmouth County, on New York and Long Branch R. R. .... Sandy Hook.

Navesink Park; seaside village in Middletown Township, Monmouth County... Sandy Hook.

Neal Branch; brook in Weymouth Township, Atlantic County, flowing into Tuckahoe River..................... Tuckahoe.

Nell Run; brook in Egg Harbor Township, Atlantic County, flowing into English Creek................................. Great Egg Harbor.

Neptune; township in Monmouth County; area, 13 square miles .... Asbury Park.

Neptune; village in Neptune Township, Monmouth County. Asbury Park.

Nescochaque; creek in Hammonton and Mullica townships, Atlantic County, flowing into Mullica River .... Mullica.

Neshanic; village in Hillsboro Township, Somerset County . Princeton.

Neshanic; river heading in Raritan and Delaware town- ⎰ Lambertville.
ships, Hunterdon County, flowing into South Branch of ⎱ Princeton.
Raritan River in Hillsboro Township, Somerset County, ⎰ Somerville.

Neshanic Station; village in Branchburg Township, Somerset County, on South Branch of Raritan River, on South Branch R. R., and on Lehigh Valley R. R.................. Somerville.

Netherwood; village, part of Plainfield City, Union County, on Green Brook, and on Central R. R. of New Jersey ..... Plainfield.

Neuvy; village in Harrington Township, Bergen County, on Northern R. R. of New Jersey............................. Tarrytown.

New Albany; village in Cinnaminson Township, Burlington County .... Burlington.

New Barbadoes; township in Bergen County; area, 4 square miles .... Paterson.

New Bedford; village in Wall Township, Monmouth County. Asbury Park.

New Bridge; village in Palisade and Englewood townships, Bergen County, on Hackensack River..................... Paterson.

New Brooklyn; village in Piscataway Township, Middlesex County, on Lehigh Valley R. R. and on Bound Brook..... Plainfield.

New Brooklyn; village in Winslow Township, Camden County, on Great Egg Harbor River .... Hammonton.

New Brunswick; city in Middlesex County, on Raritan ⎰ New Brunswick.
River and on Pennsylvania R. R. ⎱ Plainfield.

New Columbia; village in Mullica Township, Atlantic County .... Mullica.

New Dover; village in Raritan Township, Middlesex County .... Plainfield.

New Durham; village in Raritan Township, Middlesex County .... Plainfield.

New Durham; village in North Bergen Township, Hudson County, on Northern R. R. of New Jersey, West Shore R. R., and New York, Susquehanna and Western R. R....... Paterson.

New Egypt; town in Plumstead Township, Ocean County, on North Run, and on Pemberton and Hightstown R. R .. Bordentown.

New England; creek in Commercial Township, Cumberland County, flowing into Maurice River Cove................. Maurice Cove.

New England Cross Roads; village in Fairfield Township, Cumberland County .... Bridgeton.

Names of sheets.

Newfoundland; town in West Milford Township, Passaic County, on Pequannock River and on New York, Susquehanna and Western R. R .... Greenwood Lake.

New Freedom; village in Winslow Township, Camden County, on New Jersey Southern R. R..................... Mount Holly.

New Freedom; village in Upper Pittsgrove Township, Salem County .... Glassboro.

New Germantown; village in Tewksbury Township, { High Bridge.
Hunterdon County. { Somerville.

New Germany; village in Buena Vista Township, Atlantic County, on Penny Pot Stream .... Hammonton.

New Gretna; village in Bass River Township, Burlington County .... Little Egg Harbor.

New Hampton; village in Lebanon Township, Hunterdon County, on Musconetong River and on Delaware, Lackawanna and Western R. R..................................... High Bridge.

New Hanover; township in Burlington County; area, 41 { Bordentown.
square miles. { Pemberton.

New Lisbon; village in Pemberton Township, Burlington County, on Philadelphia and Long Branch R. R........... Pemberton.

New Market; village in West Amwell Township, Hunterdon County... Lambertville.

New Market; village in Piscataway Township, Middlesex County, on Lehigh Valley R. R., and on Bound Brook... Plainfield.

New Milford; village in Midland Township, Bergen County, on Hackensack River, and on New Jersey and New York R. R.. Paterson.

New Monmouth; village in Middletown Township, Monmouth County .... Sandy Hook.

New Prospect; village in Jackson Township, Ocean County. Cassville.

New Providence; village in New Providence Township, Union County....................................... Plainfield.

New Providence; township in Union County; area, 10 square miles .... Plainfield.

New Vernon; village in Passaic Township, Morris County . Plainfield.

New Village; village in Franklin Township, Warren County, on Morris Canal and on Pohatcong Creek................. Easton.

New York Upper; bay, an arm of Atlantic Ocean, separating Hudson County, N. J., New York City, and Staten Island. Staten Island.

Newark; city in Essex County on Passaic River and on { Paterson.
Newark Bay; area, 21 square miles. { Staten Island.

Newark; bay separating Hudson County from Essex and Union counties and Staten Island .... Staten Island.

Newbakers Corners; village in Hardwick Township, Warren County .... Wallpack.

Newbold; island in Delaware River in Mansfield Township, { Burlington.
Burlington County. { Bordentown.

Newbold Branch; brook in Lacey Township, Ocean County, flowing into Daniel Branch............................. Whitings.

Newbold Run; brook in New Hanover and Pemberton town- { Bordentown.
ships, Burlington County, flowing into Rancocas Creek { Pemberton.

Newell; village in Egg Harbor Township, Atlantic County, on West Jersey R. R .... Great Egg Harbor.

Newfield; village in Franklin Township, Gloucester County. Glassboro.

Names of sheets.

Newkirk; village in Upper Pittsgrove Township, Salem County, on West Jersey R. R............................ Glassboro.

Newport; town in Downe Township, Cumberland County... Bridgeton.

Newport; village in Lebanon Township, Hunterdon County, on Spruce River .... High Bridge.

Newport; creek on boundary between Stow Creek and Greenwich townships, Cumberland County, flowing into Stow Creek .... Bayside.

Newport; landing in Downe Township, Cumberland County, on Nantuxent Creek .... Bridgeton.

Newport; station in Downe Township, Cumberland County, on Nantuxent Creek .... Bridgeton.

Newton; township in Sussex County; area, 3 square miles. $\begin{cases} \text{Wallpack.} \\ \text{Franklin.} \end{cases}$

Newton; town coextensive with Newton Township, Sussex County, on Sussex R. R. $\begin{cases} \text{Franklin.} \\ \text{Wallpack.} \end{cases}$

Newton; creek in Haddon Township, Camden County; formed by three branches, Main Branch, North Branch, and South Branch, flows west into Delaware River north of Gloucester City...................................... Philadelphia.

Newton, or Pine; creek rising in Mullica Township, flows northeast, entering Egg Harbor City, Atlantic County, where it flows into Mullica River .... Mullica.

Newtonville; village in Buena Vista Township, Atlantic County. .... Hammonton.

Newtown; village in Washington Township, Mercer County. Bordentown.

Newtown; village in Piscataway Township, Middlesex County, on Ambrose Brook.............................. Plainfield.

Nicholas; channel in Middle Township, Cape May County, connecting Genesis Bay with Dung Thorofare .... Dennisville.

Nihomus Run; brook in Pilesgrove Township, Salem County, flowing into Salem Creek .... Salem.

Nishayne; brook in Montclair and Orange townships, Essex County, tributary to Second River .... Paterson.

Nishisakawick; creek in Alexandria Township, Hunterdon County, tributary to Delaware River..................... Easton.

Nixon Branch; brook in Maurice River Township, Cumberland County, tributary to Muskee Creek.................. Tuckahoe.

No More; mountain in Oxford Township, Warren County; altitude, 1,140 feet..................................... Delaware Water Gap.

No Pike; brook in Montgomery Township, Somerset County, tributary to Bedens Brook................................ Princeton.

Nolans; point of land projecting from coast of Jefferson Township, Morris County, into Lake Hopatcong, and is the southern terminus of Ogden Mine R. R.............. Lake Hopatcong.

Nordhoff; village in Englewood Township, Bergen County. Harlem.

Normahiggin; brook in Westfield and Cranford townships, Union County, tributary to Rahway River .... Plainfield.

North; hill in Shrewsbury Township, Monmouth County; elevation, 169 feet.. Sandy Hook.

North Bergen; township in Hudson County; area, 12 square miles. $\begin{cases} \text{Paterson.} \\ \text{Harlem.} \end{cases}$

North Branch; village in Branchburg Township, Somerset County, on North Branch of Raritan River.............. Somerville.

Names of sheets.

North Branch Depot; village in Branchburg Township, Somerset County, at junction of Chambers Brook with North Branch of Raritan River and on Central R. R. of New Jersey .... Somerville.

North Brunswick; township in Middlesex County; area, { New Brunswick.
14 square miles. { Princeton.

North Channel; passage in coast swamp in Middle Township, Cape May County .... Sea Isle.

North Church; village in Hardyston Township, Sussex County. Franklin.

North Long Branch; village in Ocean Township, Monmouth County, on Atlantic Ocean, and on New York and Long Branch R. R... Sandy Hook.

North Newark; village, part of Newark City, Essex County, at junction of Second River with Passaic River and where the Paterson and Newark Branch of New York, Lake Erie and Western R. r. crosses the New York and Greenwood Lake R. R .... Paterson.

North Paterson; village in Manchester Township, Passaic County .... Paterson.

North Pennsville; village in Cinnaminson Township, Burlington County, on Pensauken Creek.................... Philadelphia.

North Plainfield; township in Somerset County; area, 14 { Somerville.
square miles. { Plainfield.

North Run; brook in Springfield and New Hanover townships, Burlington County, tributary to Crosswick Creek. Bordentown.

North Vineland; village in Landis Township, Cumberland County, on West Jersey R. R............................. Glassboro.

Northampton; township in Burlington County; area, 2 { Burlington.
square miles. { Mount Holly.

Northfield; village in Livingston Township, Essex County, on Canoe Brook... Morristown.

Northville; village in Deerfield Township, Cumberland County .... Glassboro.

Norton; village in Union Township, Hunterdon County..... High Bridge.

Norton; brook in Mullica Township, Atlantic County, flowing into Hammonton Creek .... Mullica.

Nortonville; village in Logan Township, Gloucester County. Chester.

Norwood; village in Harrington Township, Bergen County, on Northern R. R. of New Jersey.......................... Harlem.

Nugentown; village in Little Egg Harbor Township, Burlington County .... Little Egg Harbor.

Nummy; swampy island in Middle Township, Cape May County .... Dennisville.

Nummytown; village in Middle Township, Cape May County .... Dennisville.

Nut Swamp; brook in Middletown Township, Monmouth County, flowing into Navesink River .... Sandy Hook.

Nutby; village in Franklin Township, Essex County, on Paterson and Newark Branch of New York, Lake Erie and Western R. R.. Paterson.

Oak; island in coast swamp in Bass River Township, Burlington County .... Little Egg Harbor.

Oak Grove; village in Franklin Township, Hunterdon County. High Bridge.

Oak Hill; village in Middletown Township, Monmouth County... Sandy Hook.

Names of sheets.

Oak Ridge; village in West Milford Township, Passaic County, on Pequannock River and on New York, Susquehanna and Western R. R .... Greenwood Lake.

Oak Tree; village in Raritan Township, Middlesex County, on Lehigh Valley R. R .... Plainfield.

Oakdale; village in Delaware Township, Hunterdon County, on Flemington Branch, Belvidere Division .... Lambertville.

Oakdale Station; village in Haddon Township, Camden County, on Philadelphia and Reading R. R .... Philadelphia.

Oakey; brook in South Brunswick Township, Middlesex County, tributary to Cow Yard Brook.................... Princeton.

Oakland; village in Upper Alloways Creek Township, Salem County, on West Jersey R. R .... Salem.

Oakland; village in Franklin Township, Bergen County, on New York, Susquehanna and Western R. R .... Ramapo.

Oakland Mills; village in Manalapan Township, Monmouth County .... Cassville.

Oakville; village in Weymouth Township, Atlantic County. Tuckahoe.

Obhonan Ridgway Branch; brook in Jackson Township, Ocean County, flowing into Ridgway Branch............ Cassville.

Ocean; township in Ocean County; area, 34 square miles .. { Whitings. / Barnegat.

Ocean; township in Monmouth County; area, 25 square miles { Asbury Park. / Sandy Hook. / Long Beach.

Ocean; county in east central part of the State; area, 676 square miles. { Bordentown. / Pemberton. / Cassville. / Asbury Park. / Whitings. / Barnegat. / Little Egg Harbor. / Long Beach.

Ocean Beach; borough in Wall Township, Monmouth County, on New York and Long Branch R. R. and on Atlantic coast .... Asbury Park.

Ocean City; borough on coast of Cape May County......... Great Egg Harbor.

Ocean City; life-saving station at Ocean City .... Great Egg Harbor.

Ocean Grove; town and summer resort in Neptune Township, Monmouth County, on New York and Long Branch R. R. and on Atlantic ocean .... Asbury Park.

Ocean Park; village in Neptune Township, Monmouth County Asbury Park.

Ocean View; village in Dennis Township, Cape May County, on West Jersey R. R .... Sea Isle.

Oceanic; towns in Shrewsbury Township, Monmouth County, on Navesink River....................................... Sandy Hook.

Oceanport; village in Eatontown Township, Monmouth County... Sandy Hook.

Oceanville; village in Galloway Township, Atlantic County. Atlantic City.

Ogden; village in West Deptford Township, Gloucester County, on West Jersey R. R............................. Philadelphia.

Ogden; creek in Fairfield Township, Cumberland County, tributary to Back Creek. { Bridgeton. / Bayside.

Ogden; creek in Downe Township, Cumberland County, flowing into Dividing Creek. { Bridgeton. / Maurice Cove.

Names of sheets.

Ogdensburg; village in Sparta Township, Sussex County, on Sussex R. R., and on New York, Susquehanna and Western R. R .... Franklin.

Old; light-house on coast of Greenwich Township, Cumberland County .... Bayside.

Old Boonton; village in Hanover Township, Morris County, on Rockaway River .... Morristown.

Old Bridge; village in East Brunswick Township, Middlesex County, on South River, and on Camden and Amboy Branch Pennsylvania R. R .... New Brunswick.

Old Church; village in Monroe Township, Middlesex County. New Brunswick.

Old Half Way; village in Manchester Township, Ocean County .... Whitings

Old Hatch; creek in Fairfield Township, Cumberland County, flowing into Back Creek .... Bayside.

Old Hurricane; brook in Manchester Township, Ocean County, flowing into Union Branch of Toms River. { Cassville. Whitings.

Old Robin; brook in Dennis Township, Cape May County, tributary to Dennis Creek .... Dennisville.

Old Sams; pond in Brick Township, Ocean County .... Asbury Park.

Old Turtle Thorofare; passage in coast swamp in Middle Township, Cape May County .... Dennisville.

Oldham; brook rising in Franklin Township, Bergen County, flows through Manchester Township, Passaic County, and Paterson City, thence into Passaic River .... Paterson.

Oldman; creek rising in South Harrison Township, Gloucester County, flowing northwest on boundary between Gloucester and Salem counties, into Delaware River. { Salem. Glassboro.

Oldman; creek in Middle Township, Cape May County, flowing into Great Channel .... Dennisville.

Oldman; creek on boundary between Salem and Gloucester counties, flowing into Delaware River .... Chester.

Oldman; township in Salem County; area, 21 square miles . Salem.

Oldman; point projecting from Oldman Township, Salem County, into Delaware River .... Chester.

Ongs Hat; village in Pemberton Township, Burlington County .... Pemberton.

Ongs Run; brook in Pemberton Township, Burlington County, flowing into Newbold Run .... Pemberton.

Oradell; village in Midland Township, Bergen County, on Hackensack River and on New Jersey and New York R. R. Paterson.

Orange; city in Essex County, on Orange Branch of New York and Greenwood Lake R. R., and on Morris and Essex Division Delaware Lackawanna and Western R. R. { Paterson. Morristown.

Orange Valley; village, part of Orange City, Essex County, on Morris and Essex Division, Delaware, Lackawanna and Western R. R .... Paterson.

Oranoaken; creek in Downe Township, Cumberland County, flowing into Maurice River Cove. { Bridgeton. Maurice Cove.

Ore Spring; brook in Woodland and Shamong townships, Burlington County, flowing into Feather Bed Brook ..... Pemberton.

Ortley; village on reef in Dover Township, Ocean County, on Philadelphia and Long Branch R. R .... Barnegat.

Orvil; township in Bergen County; area, 17 square miles... { Paterson. Ramapo.

Names of sheets.

Osborne; island in Manasquan River off coast of Brick Township, Ocean County .... Asbury Park.

Osborne; island in coast swamp in Little Egg Harbor Township, Burlington County .... Little Egg Harbor.

Oswego; river in Ocean and Burlington counties, tributary to Wading River. 〈 Whitings.
Little Egg Harbor.
Mullica.

Otter; brook in Center and Gloucester townships, Camden County, tributary to North Branch of Timber Creek..... Philadelphia.

Overpeck; creek rising in Palisade Township, flows west into Hackensack River in Ridgefield Township, Bergen County. 〈 Paterson.
Harlem.

Overton; village in Palisade Township, Bergen County, on Hackensack River and on New Jersey and New York R. R. Paterson.

Oxford; township in Warren County; area, 34 square miles. 〈 Delaware Water Gap.
Hackettstown.

Oxford Church; village in Oxford Township, Warren County, on Pophandusing Brook. P. O. Hazen.................... Delaware Water Gap,

Oxford Furnace; town in Oxford Township, Warren County, on Delaware, Lackawanna and Western R. R. 〈 Delaware Water Gap.
Hackettstown.

Oyster; creek in coast swamp in Downe Township, Cumberland County .... Maurice Cove.

Oyster; creek rising in Ocean Township, flows northeast, forming partial boundary between Lacey and Ocean townships, Ocean County, into Barnegat Bay. 〈 Whitings.
Barnegat.

Oyster; creek in Elizabeth City, tributary to Newark Bay... Staten Island.

Oyster; creek in Middle Township, Cape May County, flowing into Cresse Thorofare............................... Dennisville.

Oyster; cove projecting from Delaware River into Lower Alloways Creek Township, Salem County.................. Bayside.

Oyster Thorofare; passage in coast swamp in Galloway Township, Atlantic County............................... Atlantic City.

Pavonia; village in Stockton Township, Camden County, on Delaware River, at junction of Amboy Division with Pennsylvania R. R .... Philadelphia.

Packer; island in South Branch of Raritan River between Readington and Raritan townships, Hunterdon County. High Bridge.

Paddy Thorofare; passage in coast swamp in Middle Township, Cape May County .... Dennisville.

Padgett; creek in Downe Township, Cumberland County, flowing into Delaware River .... Bridgeton.

Pahaquarry; township in Warren County; area, 21 square miles. 〈 Wallpack.
Bushkill Falls.
Delaware Water Gap.

Paint Branch; brook in Manchester Township, Ocean County, flowing into Manapaqua Branch.......................... Cassville.

Palmyra; town in Cinnaminson Township, Burlington County, on Pennsylvania R. R............................. Philadelphia.

Palatine; village in Pittsgrove Township, Salem County, on West Jersey R. R... Glassboro.

Palermo; village in Upper Township, Cape May County..... Great Egg Harbor.

Palisade; township in Bergen County; area, 16 square miles. 〈 Harlem.
Paterson.

Palmyra; village in Alexandria Township, Hunterdon County. Easton.

Names of sheets.

Pamrapo; part of Bayonne City, on New York Upper Bay and on Central R. R. of New Jersey.......................... Staten Island.

Pancoast Branch; brook in Maurice River Township, Cumberland County, tributary to Muskee Creek............... Tuckahoe.

Pancoast Mill; village in Buena Vista Township, Atlantic County, on Deep Run.. Hammonton.

Panther; pond in Byram Township, Sussex County........ Lake Hopatcong.

Panther Branch; brook in Buena Vista Township, Atlantic County, and Landis Township, Cumberland County, tributary to Manantico Creek...................................... Tuckahoe.

Papakating; village in Wantage Township, Sussex County, on New York, Susquehanna and Western R. R............. Franklin.

Papakating; village in Frankford Township, Sussex County, on Papakating Creek....................................... Franklin.

Papakating; creek in Frankford and Wantage townships, Sussex County, flowing into Wallkill River............. Franklin.

Pappoose Branch; brook rising in Woodland Township, flows southwest, forming boundary between Randolph and Bass River townships, into Oswego River. } Whitings. Little Egg Harbor.

Paradise; village in West Deptford Township, Gloucester County, on Delaware River R. R........................... Philadelphia.

Paradise; village in Upper Freehold Township, Monmouth County... Cassville.

Paramus; village in Ridgewood Township, Bergen County, on Saddle River... Paterson.

Park Ridge; village in Washington Township, Bergen County, on New Jersey and New York R. R....................... Ramapo.

Parkdale; village in Waterford Township, Camden County on New Jersey Southern R. R............................... Hammonton.

Parker; mine situated in central part of Vermont Township, Sussex County... Greenwood Lake.

Parker; creek in Shrewsbury and Eatontown townships, Monmouth County, flowing into Shrewsbury River...... Sandy Hook.

Parker; creek in Mount Laurel Township, on boundary between Mount Laurel and Chester townships, Burlington County, flowing into Rancocas Creek................. Mount Holly.

Parker; island in Little Egg Harbor, Eagleswood Township, Ocean County... Long Beach.

Parker; island in Little Egg Harbor, in Little Egg Harbor Township, Burlington County............................ Little Egg Harbor.

Parker; cove projecting from Little Egg Harbor into Eagleswood Township, Ocean County............................ Little Egg Harbor.

Parker; brook in Little Egg Harbor Township, Burlington County, and Eagleswood Township, Ocean County, flowing into Parker Cove....................................... Little Egg Harbor.

Parkertown; village in Little Egg Harbor Township, Burlington County, on Tuckahoe R. R....................... Little Egg Harbor.

Parkville; village in West Deptford Township, Gloucester County, on West Jersey R. R............................... Philadelphia.

Parry; village in Cinnaminson Township, Burlington County. Burlington.

Parsippany; town in Hanover Township, Morris County, on Troy Brook.. Morristown.

Parsonage Run; brook in Deerfield Township, Cumberland County, flowing into Foster Run. } Glassboro. Bridgeton.

Names of sheets.

Parvin Branch; brook on boundary between Bridgeton and Fairfield townships, Cumberland County, flowing into Cohansey Creek .... Bridgeton.

Parvin Branch; brook in Landis Township, Cumberland County, flowing into Maurice River .... Bridgeton

Pascock; creek in Rockland and Washington townships, Bergen County, flowing into Hackensack River. { Ramapo. Paterson. Harlem.

Passaic; county in northeast part of the State; area, 200 square miles. { Greenwood Lake. Ramapo. Morristown. Paterson.

Passaic; township in Morris County; area, 33 square miles. { Morristown. Plainfield. Somerville. Lake Hopatcong.

Passaic; city in Passaic County............................. Paterson.

Passaic; river in northern New Jersey, flows into Newark Bay at Newark. { Lake Hopatcong. Somerville. Plainfield. Morristown. Paterson. Staten Island.

Passaic Bridge; part of Passaic City, on Passaic River where the New York, Lake Erie and Western R. R. crosses the river .... Paterson.

Patcong; creek in Egg Harbor Township, Atlantic County, flowing into Great Egg Harbor........................... Great Egg Harbor.

Paterson; city in Passaic County, on Passaic River, and on Morris Canal; area, 8 square miles...................... Paterson.

Pattenburg; village in Union Township, Hunterdon County, on Lehigh Valley R. R............................... Easton.

Paulding; village in Pilesgrove Township, Salem County, on West Jersey R. R...................................... Salem.

Paulina; village in Blairstown Township, Warren County, on Paulins Kill and on New York, Susquehanna and Western R. R....................................... Hackettstown.

Paulins Kill; river in Sussex and Warren counties, flowing into Delaware River. { Franklin. Hackettstown. Wallpack. Delaware Water Gap.

Paulsboro; town in Greenwich Township, Gloucester County, on Mantua Creek and on Delaware River R. R .. Philadelphia.

Peapack; brook heading in Chester Township, Morris County, flows into North Branch of Raritan River in Bedminster Township, Somerset County.................. Somerville.

Peapack; village in Bedminister Township, Somerset County, on Peapack Brook .... Somerville.

Peck; beach on coast of Upper Township, Cape May County. { Sea Isle. Great Egg Harbor.

Peck; bay in Upper Township, Cape May County, flows into Great Egg Harbor .... Great Egg Harbor

Peck Beach; life-saving station on coast of Upper Township, Cape May County.. Sea Isle.

Pecks Corner; village in Quinton Township, Salem County. Salem.

Names of sheets.

Peckman; brook rising in West Orange Township, flows through Caldwell Township, Essex County, into Passaic River in Little Falls Township, Passaic County .... Paterson.

Pedricktown; village in Oldman Township, Salem County.. Chester.

Pemberton; township in Burlington County; area, 65 square miles.
{ Pemberton.
{ Whitings.
{ Bordentown.

Pemberton; borough in Pemberton Township, Burlington County, on Rancocas Creek and on Camden and New Jersey Southern railroads .... Pemberton.

Penbyrn; village in Winslow Township, Camden County ... Mount Holly.

Penhorn; creek in North Bergen Township, Hudson County, tributary to Hackensack River................ .... Paterson.

Penn Place; village in Randolph Township, Burlington County.. Little Egg Harbor.

Pennington; town in Hopewell Township, Mercer County, on New York Division, Philadelphia and Reading R. R .. Lambertville.

Pennington; island off coast of Kingwood Township, Hunterdon County, in Delaware River.......... .... Easton.

Pennsgrove; borough in Upper Penns Neck Township, Salem County, on Delaware River........................... Salem.

Penns Neck; village in West Windsor Township, Mercer County, on Pennsylvania R. R............. .... Princeton.

Pennsville; village in Lower Penns Neck Township, Salem County .... Wilmington.

Penny Pot Stream; brook.in Winslow Township, Camden County, and Hammonton and Buena Vista townships, Atlantic County, flows into Great Egg Harbor River.... Hammonton.

Pensauken: creek formed by North and South Branch, rising in Burlington County, flows northwest on boundary between Burlington and Camden counties into Delaware River.
{ Philadelphia.
{ Mount Holly.

Pensauken Station; village in Stockton Township, Camden County, on Pensylvania R. R., Amboy Division........ .... Philadelphia.

Penton; village in Mannington Township, Salem County, on West Jersey R. R .... Salem.

Penville; village in Mansfield Township, Warren County, on Musconetong River .... Hackettstown

Pequannock; village in Pequannock Township, Morris County, on Pompton River and on New York and Greenwood Lake R. R .... Morristown.

Pequannock; township in Morris County; area, 37 square miles.
{ Greenwood Lake.
{ Morristown.

Pequannock; river heading in Hardiston Township, Sussex County, forms boundary between Passaic and Morris counties, and joins the Wanaque River at Pompton, and together they form the Pompton River.
{ Franklin.
{ Greenwood Lake.
{ Morristown.

Pequest; river heading in Greenwich Township, Sussex County, flowing southwest through Warren County into the Delaware River at Belvidere.
{ Wallpack.
{ Hackettstown.
{ Delaware Water Gap.

Pequest Furnace; village in Oxford Township, Warren County, on Pequest River, and on Delaware, Lackawanna and Western R. R., and Lehigh and Hudson River R. R... Hackettstown.

Names of sheets.

Perch, cove projecting from Little Bay in Galloway Township, Atlantic County...... Atlantic City.

Perch Cove Run; brook in Egg Harbor Township, Atlantic County, flowing into Great Egg Harbor River...... Great Egg Harbor.

Perkintown; station in Oldman Township, Salem County, on Delaware River R. R...... Salem.

Perkintown; village in Oldman Township, Salem County.. Salem.

Perrineville; village in Millstone Township, Monmouth County...... Cassville.

Perryville; village in Union Township, Hunterdon County.. High Bridge.

Perth Amboy; city and township coextensive; Middlesex County, on Raritan Bay at mouth of Raritan River and at south end of Arthur Kill or Staten Island Sound...... Plainfield.

Peru; village in Acquackanonck Township, Passaic County, on Paterson and Newark Branch of New York, Lake Erie and Western R. R...... Paterson.

Pestletown; village in Waterford Township, Camden County. Hammonton.

Peters; brook in Bridgewater Township, Somerset County, tributary to Raritan River...... Somerville.

Peters; creek in Haddon Township, Camden County, tributary to Newton Creek...... Philadelphia.

Petersburg; village in Jefferson Township, Morris County... Franklin.

Petersburg; village in Upper Township, Cape May County.. Great Egg Harbor.

Petersburg; village in Independence Township, Warren County...... Hackettstown.

Petit; island in Manahawken Bay, in Stafford Township, Ocean County...... Long Beach.

Petticoat; brook in Millville Township, Cumberland County, flowing into Maurice River...... Bridgeton.

Pews; creek in Middletown Township, Monmouth County, flowing into Sandy Hook Bay...... Sandy Hook.

Phalanx; village in Atlantic Township, Monmouth County. Sandy Hook.

Phillip; creek in Greenwich Township, Cumberland County, flowing into Stow Creek...... Bayside.

Phillipsburg; city in Warren County, on Delaware River at western terminus of Morris Canal...... Easton.

Piermont; village in Middle Township, Cape May County.. Sea Isle.

Pier Point Neck; peninsula at south part of Fairfield Township, Cumberland County...... Bayside.

Pierce Point; village on coast of Middle Township, Cape May County...... Dennisville.

Pierson; creek in Newark City, Essex County, tributary to Maple Island Creek...... Staten Island.

Pigeon; swamp in South Brunswick Township, Middlesex County...... Princeton.

Pilesgrove; township in Salem County; area, 37 square miles...... Salem.

Pimple; hills in Sparta Township, Sussex County...... Franklin.

Pine; creek rising in Mullica Township, flows northeast, entering Egg Harbor City, Atlantic County, where it flows into Mullica River...... Mullica.

Pine; brook tributary to Matchaponix Brook, in Marlboro and Manalapan townships, Monmouth County...... New Brunswick.

Names of sheets.

Pine; brook on boundary between Atlantic and Shrewsbury townships, Monmouth County, flows through Shrewsbury Township into Swimming River .... Sandy Hook.

Pine; brook in Caldwell Township, Essex County, tributary to Passaic River .... Morristown.

Pine; swamp in Sparta Township, Sussex County .... Franklin.

Pine; swamp in Montgomery Township, Sussex County..... Port Jervis.

Pine Branch; brook in Landis Township, Cumberland County, flowing into Blackwater Branch................. Glassboro.

Pine Branch; village in Montville Township, Morris County, on Passaic River.. Morristown.

Pine Brook; village in Shrewsbury Township, Monmouth County .... Sandy Hook.

Pine Mount; creek in Greenwich Township, Cumberland County, flowing into Cohansey Creek.................... Bayside.

Piney Hollow; village in Franklin Township, Gloucester County .... Hammonton.

Pinkneyville; village in Andover Township, Sussex County. Franklin.

Piper Corner; village in Medford Township, Burlington County .... Mount Holly.

Piscataway; township in Middlesex County; area, 32 square miles. { Plainfield. Somerville.

Piscataway; village in Raritan Township, Middlesex County. Plainfield.

Pitman Grove; village in Mantua Township, Gloucester County .... Glassboro.

Pittstown; village in Franklin and Alexandria townships, Hunterdon County....................................... High Bridge.

Pittsgrove; township in Salem County; area, 50 square miles. { Bridgeton. Glassboro.

Pittsgrove; village in Upper Pittsgrove Township, Salem County .... Glassboro.

Plainfield; city in Union County .... Plainfield.

Plainfield; borough in Montgomery Township, Somerset County .... Princeton.

Plainville; village in Franklin Township, Gloucester County. Glassboro.

Plainsboro; village in Cranberry Township, Middlesex County .... Princeton.

Pleasant; run in Readington Township, Hunterdon County, and Branchburg Township, Somerset County, flows into South Branch of Raritan River. } High Bridge. Somerville.

Pleasant Grove; village in Washington Township, Morris County... Hackettstown.

Pleasant Grove; village in Jackson Township, Ocean County. Cassville.

Pleasant Grove; village in Deerfield Township, Cumberland County... Bridgeton.

Pleasant Mills; village in Washington Township, Burlington County, on Mullica River .... Mullica.

Pleasant Plains; village in Passaic Township, Morris County, on Black Brook .... Plainfield.

Pleasant Run; village in Readington Township, Hunterdon County, on Pleasant Run .... High Bridge.

Pleasant Valley; village in Washington Township, Warren County. .... Delaware Water Gap.

Pleasant View; village in Hillsboro Township, Somerset County, on Philadelphia and Reading R. R.............. Princeton.

96   A GEOGRAPHIC DICTIONARY OF NEW JERSEY.

Pleasantdale; village in West Orange Township, Essex County .... Morristown.

Pleasantville; village in Landis Township, Cumberland County .... Glassboro.

Pleasantville; borough in Egg Harbor Township, Atlantic County, on West Jersey R. R .... Great Egg Harbor.

Pleasantville; village in Passaic Township, Morris County.. Plainfield.

Pleasure; bay, an enlargement of Pleasure Bay River, in Eatontown Township, Monmouth County .... Sandy Hook.

Pleasure Bay; river on boundary between Eatontown and Ocean townships, Monmouth County .... Sandy Hook.

Pluckamin; village in Bridgewater Township, Somerset County .... Somerville.

Plumbsock; village in Wantage Township, Sussex County, on Western Branch of Papakating Creek .... Franklin.

Plumstead; township in Ocean County; area, 40 square miles. { Whitings. Cassville. Bordentown.

Pohatcong; township in Warren County; area, 15 square miles .... Easton.

Pohatcong; creek in Independence, Mansfield, Washington, Franklin, Greenwich, and Pohatcong townships, Warren County, flowing into Delaware River. { Hackettstown. Delaware Water Gap. Easton.

Pohatcong; mountain ridge extending from Washington Township, through center of Franklin Township into Greenwich Township, Warren County .... Easton.

Point, The; village in Lebanon Township, Hunterdon County, on Musconetcong River .... Hackettstown.

Point Airy; village in Pilesgrove Township, Salem County.. Salem.

Point Airy; station in Pilesgrove Township, Salem County, on West Jersey R. R .... Salem.

Point Pleasant; borough in Brick Township, Ocean County. Asbury Park.

Point Pleasant; village in Gloucester Township, Camden County .... Philadelphia.

Pointville; village in New Hanover Township, Burlington County .... Bordentown.

Pole Branch; brook in Woodland Township, Burlington County, tributary to Gates Branch of Wading River..... Pemberton.

Pole Bridge; brook in Manchester Township, Ocean County, and Pemberton Township, Burlington County, tributary to Mount Misery Brook. { Whitings. Pemberton.

Pole Bridge Branch; brook in Weymouth Township, Atlantic County, flowing into Tuckahoe River .... Tuckahoe.

Polhemus Branch; brook in Dover Township, Ocean County, tributary to Kettle Creek .... Asbury Park.

Polipod; brook in Howell Township, Monmouth County, flowing into Hay Stack Brook .... Asbury Park.

Polktown; village in Union Township, Hunterdon County.. High Bridge.

Polkville; village in Knowlton Township, Warren County.. Delaware Water Gap.

Pomona; village in Galloway Township, Atlantic County, on Camden and Atlantic R. R .... Great Egg Harbor.

Pompeston; creek in Chester and Cinnaminson townships, Burlington County, flowing into Delaware River. { Burlington. Germantown. Mount Holly.

Names of sheets.

Pompton; township in Passaic County; area, 53 square miles. { Greenwood Lake. Ramapo. Morristown.

Pompton; river formed by Wanaque and Pequannock rivers, which unite at Pompton. It forms boundary between Morris and Passaic counties, and flows into Passaic River at Two Bridges. } Franklin. Greenwood Lake. Morristown.

Pompton; lake in Pompton Township, Passaic County...... { Greenwood Lake. Morristown.

Pompton; village in Pompton Township, Passaic County.... Morristown.

Pompton Junction; village in Pompton Township, Passaic County .... Greenwood Lake.

Pompton Plains; village in Pequannock Township, Morris County, on Pompton River and on New York and Greenwood Lake R. R .... Morristown.

Pond; creek in Lower Township, Cape May County, flowing into Delaware Bay.. Cape May.

Pond Run; village in Pond Run, in Hamilton Township, Mercer County... Bordentown.

Pond Run; brook in Hamilton Township, Mercer County, flowing into Assanpink Creek .... Bordentown.

Pope; brook in Springfield Township, Union County, tributary to East Branch of Rahway River .... Plainfield.

Popes Branch; brook tributary to Long Cripple, Woodland Township, Burlington County................................. Whitings.

Pophandusing; brook in Oxford Township, Warren County, flowing into Delaware River at Belvidere................. Delaware Water Gap.

Poplar; village in Ocean Township, Monmouth County ..... Sandy Hook.

Poplar; hill in Raritan Township, Middlesex County; altitude, 235 feet .... Plainfield.

Popular; point projecting from Stafford Township, Ocean County, into Little Egg Harbor............................ Long Beach.

Porch; branch of Mantua Creek, in Washington Township, Gloucester County. { Philadelphia. Glassboro.

Porchtown; village in Franklin Township, Gloucester County, near junction of Little Ease Run and Still Run, tributaries of Maurice River................................. Glassboro.

Poricy; brook in Middletown Township, Monmouth County, flowing into Navesink River .... Sandy Hook.

Port Colden; village in Washington Township, Warren County, on Morris Canal and on Delaware, Lackawanna and Western R. R .... Hackettstown.

Port Elizabeth; village in Maurice River Township, Cumberland County, on West Jersey R. R........................... Tuckahoe.

Port Mercer; village in West Windsor Township, Mercer County, on Delaware and Raritan Canal.................. Princeton.

Port Monmouth; village in Middletown Township, Monmouth County, on Sandy Hook Bay .... Sandy Hook.

Port Morris; village in Roxbury Township, Morris County, on Morris Canal and on Delaware, Lackawanna and Western R. R... Lake Hopatcong.

Port Murray; village in Mansfield Township, Warren County, on Morris Canal and on Delaware, Lackawanna and Western R. R.. Hackettstown.

Bull. 118——7

Names of sheets.

Port Norris; village in Commercial Township, Cumberland County .... Maurice Cove.

Port Oram; town in Randolph Township, Morris County, on Rockaway River and on Morris Canal .... Lake Hopatcong

Port Republic; village in Galloway Township, Atlantic County .... Little Egg Harbor.

Port Warren; village in Lopatcong Township, Warren County, on Morris Canal and on Lopatcong Creek................. Easton.

Portage; lake in Pompton Township, Passaic County, N. J., and Rockland County, N. Y............................... Ramapo.

Post; creek in Lower Township, Cape May County........... Cape May.

Post; island in swamp in Independence Township, Warren County .... Hackettstown.

Post; brook in West Milford and Pompton townships, Passaic County, tributary to Wanaque River................. Greenwood Lake.

Postville; village in West Milford Township, Passaic County   Greenwood Lake.

Potter; creek in Berkeley Township, Ocean County, flowing into Barnegat Bay .... Barnegat.

Potterstown; village in Readington Township, Hunterdon County .... High Bridge

Pottersville; village in Bedminster Township, Somerset County, on Lamington River.............................. Somerville.

Poverty; beach on coast of Lower Township, Cape May County .... Cape May.

Powell; creek in Egg Harbor Township, Atlantic County, flowing into Great Egg Harbor River...................... Great Egg Harbor.

Powerville; village in Boonton Township, Morris County, on Morris Canal and on Rockaway River.................. Morristown.

Prattsville; village in Delaware Township, Hunterdon County, on Wickecheoke Creek .... Lambertville.

Preakness; village in Wayne Township, Passaic County, on Preakness Brook... Paterson.

Preakness; brook in Wayne Township, Passaic County, { Paterson. tributary to Pompton River. { Morristown.

Preakness; mountain, a division of the Second Watchung Mountain, in Wayne Township, Passaic County.......... Paterson.

Prescott; brook in Clinton Township, Hunterdon County, tributary to South Branch of Raritan River............. High Bridge.

Price Branch; brook in Waterford Township, Camden County. Hammonton.

Primrose; brook in Passaic Township, Morris County, tribu- { Somerville. tary to Passaic River. { Lake Hopatcong.

Princeton; township in Mercer County; area, 18 square miles. Princeton.

Princeton; borough in Princeton Township, Mercer County, on Pennsylvania R. R.................................... Princeton.

Princeton Junction; village in West Windsor Township, Mercer County, at junction of Princeton Branch of Pennsylvania R. R... Princeton.

Princesville; village in Lawrence Township, Mercer County. Princeton

Prospect; village in Logan Township, Gloucester County, on Delaware River R. R..................................... Chester.

Prospect Plains; village in Cranbury Township, Middlesex County, on Camden and Amboy R. R., Pennsylvania R. R. New Brunswick.

Prospertown; village in Upper Freehold Township, Monmouth County, on Lahaway Creek...................... Cassville.

Names of sheets.

Prossers Mills; village in Gloucester Township, Camden County, on South Branch of Timber Creek............... Philadelphia.

Pullen; island in coast swamp in Galloway Township, Atlantic County.. Atlantic City.

Pump Branch; brook in Winslow and Waterford townships, Camden County, tributary to Albertson Brook............ Hammonton.

Pursey; brook tributary to Repaupo Creek, in Greenwich Township, Gloucester County.............................. Chester.

Quaker; village in Washington Township, Burlington County, on Batsto River.................................... Mullica.

Quakertown; village in Franklin Township, Hunterdon County.. High Bridge.

Quick; pond in Stillwater Township, Sussex County, extending into Hampton Township, Sussex County.............. Wallpack.

Quinton; township in Salem County; area, 25 square miles.. { Bayside. / Salem.

Quinton; town in Quinton Township, Salem County......... Salem.

Raccoon; creek flowing through Gloucester County into Delaware River .... Chester.

Raccoon; creek in Harrison and Woolwich townships, Gloucester County, flowing into Delaware River............. Salem.

Raccoon; island in Delaware River off coast of Logan Township, Gloucester County .... Chester.

Raccoon; island off western coast of Jefferson Township, Morris County, and eastern coast of Byram Township, Sussex County, in Lake Hopatcong .... Lake Hopatcong.

Race; canal in Randolph Township, Burlington County, connects Oswego River, or East Branch of Wading River, with West Branch of Wading River........................... Mullica.

Radix; village in Monroe Township, Gloucester County, on Philadelphia and Reading R. R............................. Hammonton.

Rahway; city in Union County, on Rahway River and on Pennsylvania R. R .... Plainfield.

Rahway; river heading in West Orange Township, Essex { Staten Island. / County, flows through Union County into Arthur Kill, { Plainfield. / south of Linden Township. { Morristown.

Rahway, East Branch of; river in Essex and Union counties, tributary to Rahway River. { Plainfield. / Morristown.

Rahway, South Branch of; river rising in Middlesex County, flows into Rahway River in Rahway City, Union County. Plainfield.

Rail Swamp Branch; brook in Burlington and Ocean counties, flowing into Westecunk Creek .... Little Egg Harbor.

Rainbow; group of islands in Great Egg Harbor, in Upper Township, Cape May County .... Great Egg Harbor.

Rainbow Thorofare; passage in Rainbow Islands, in Upper Township, Cape May County........................... Great Egg Harbor.

Ramapo; mountain range in Bergen and Passaic counties, { Greenwood Lake. / and extending into New York. { Ramapo.

Ramapo; river rising in Orange County, N. Y., flowing { Ramapo. / through Bergen, Passaic, and Wayne counties, N. J., into { Greenwood Lake. / Pompton River. { Morristown.

Rambo; station on Delaware River R. R., in Greenwich Township, Gloucester County .... Chester.

Ramsey; village in Hohokus Township, Bergen County, on New York, Lake Erie and Western R. R................. Ramapo.

Names of sheets.

Ramseyburg; village in Knowlton Township, Warren County, on Delaware River and on Delaware, Lackawanna and Western R. R... Delaware Water Gap.

Rancocas; village in West Hampton and Willingboro townships, Burlington County.................................... Burlington.

Rancocas; creek heading in two branches, the North Branch and the South Branch, flowing northwest across Burlington County into Delaware River.
{ Whitings.
Mount Holly.
Pemberton.
Burlington.

Randell; village in Harrington Township, Bergen County, on West Shore R. R...................................... Harlem.

Randolph; township in Burlington County; area, 62 square miles.
{ Pemberton.
Whitings.
Little Egg Harbor.
Mullica.

Randolph; township in Morris County; area, 28 square miles. Lake Hopatcong.

Raritan; township in Monmouth County; area, 9 square miles .... Sandy Hook.

Raritan; township in Middlesex County; area, 36 square miles.
{ Plainfield.
New Brunswick.

Raritan; township in Hunterdon County; area, 40 square miles.
{ High Bridge.
Lambertville.

Raritan; borough in Bridgewater Township, Somerset County, on Raritan River and on Central R. R. of New Jersey .... Somerville.

Raritan; bay between Staten Island and mainland of New Jersey .... Sandy Hook.

Raritan; river formed by two branches, the North and South branches, in Morris, Somerset, and Middlesex counties, flowing into Raritan Bay.
{ Lake Hopatcong.
Hackettstown.
High Bridge.
Somerville.
Plainfield.
New Brunswick.

Raven Rock; village in Delaware Township, Hunterdon County, on Delaware River and on Belvidere Division, Pennsylvania R. R....................................... Doylestown.

Readingsburg; village in High Bridge Township, Hunterdon County, on South Branch of Raritan River, and on High Bridge Branch of Central R. R. of New Jersey........... High Bridge.

Readington; township in Hunterdon County; area, 49 square miles.
{ High Bridge.
Somerville.

Readington; village in Readington Township, Hunterdon County, on Hollands Brook............................... Somerville.

Reaville; village in East Amwell and Raritan townships, Hunterdon County.. Lambertville.

Recklesstown; village in Chesterfield Township, Burlington County .... Bordentown.

Red; hill in Chesterfield Township, Burlington County; elevation, 234 feet .... Bordentown.

Red Bank; town in Shrewsbury Township, Monmouth County, at junction of New York and Long Branch R. R., and Atlantic Highlands Branch of New Jersey Southern R. R... Sandy Hook.

Red Bank; village in West Deptford Township, Gloucester County, on Delaware River........................... Philadelphia.

Names of sheets.

Red Lion; village in Southampton Township, Burlington County .... Pemberton.

Red Oak Grove; village in Lacey Township, Ocean County. Whitings.

Red Tavern; village in Monroe Township, Middlesex County. New Brunswick.

Red Valley; village in Upper Freehold Township, Monmouth County .... Cassville.

Reding; pond in Andover Township, Sussex County......... Wallpack.

Reed; island in Little Egg Harbor, in Stafford Township, Ocean County .... Long Beach.

Reed; bay in coast swamp in Galloway Township, Atlantic County .... Atlantic City.

Reeves; village in Medford Township, Burlington County, on Medford Branch R. R....................................... Mount Holly.

Repaupo; village in Woolwich Township, Gloucester County. Chester.

Repaupo; creek on boundary between Greenwich Township on the east and Logan and Woolwich townships on the west, Gloucester County...................................... Chester.

Retreat; village in Southampton Township, Burlington County .... Pemberton.

Rhode Hall; village in South Brunswick Township, Middlesex County... New Brunswick.

Richardson; channel connecting Richardson Sound, in Middle Township, with Turtle Gut Inlet in Lower Township, Cape May County. } Cape May. Dennisville.

Richardson; sound in Middle Township, Cape May County.. Dennisville.

Richfield; village in Acquackanonck Township, Passaic County, on Morris Canal................................... Paterson.

Richland; village in Buena Vista Township, Atlantic County. Tuckahoe.

Richmanville; village in Pilesgrove Township, Salem County, on Salem coast...................................... Salem.

Riddleton; village in Upper Alloways Creek Township, Salem County, on West Jersey R. R............................ Salem.

Ridgefield; township in Bergen County; area, 19 square miles. } Harlem. Paterson.

Ridgefield; village in Ridgefield Township, Bergen County, on Northern R. R. of New Jersey......................... Paterson.

Ridgefield Park; village in Ridgefield Township, Bergen County, on Hackensack River............................. Paterson.

Ridgeway; station in Manchester Township, Ocean County, on New Jersey Southern R. R............................ Cassville.

Ridgeway Branch; brook in Jackson and Manchester townships, Ocean County, tributary to Union Branch of Toms River.. Cassville.

Ridgewood; township in Bergen County; area, 7 square miles. } Paterson. Ramapo.

Ridgewood; town in Ridgewood Township, Bergen County, on New York, Lake Erie and Western R. R............... Paterson.

Riggan; ditch in Maurice River Township, Cumberland County, flowing into Delaware Bay.................... Dennisville.

Ringoes; village in East Amwell Township, Hunterdon County .... Lambertville.

Ringwood; village in Pompton Township, Passaic County, on Ringwood Creek and on Ringwood Branch of New York and Greenwood Lake R. R........,....................... Greenwood Lake.

102   A GEOGRAPHIC DICTIONARY OF NEW JERSEY.

Names of sheets.

Ringwood; creek heading in Orange County, N. Y., and flowing into Wanaque River in Pompton Township, Passaic County. ..... Greenwood Lake.

Rio Grande; village in Middle Township, Cape May County, on West Jersey R. R ..... Dennisville.

Risley; channel in coast swamp in Egg Harbor Township, Atlantic County, flowing into Great Egg Harbor ..... Great Egg Harbor.

Risley Branch; brook in Woodland Township, Burlington County, tributary to Governors Hill Brook ..... Pemberton.

Risleyville; village in Egg Harbor Township, Atlantic County ..... Great Egg Harbor.

River Edge; village in Midland Township, Bergen County, on Hackensack River and on New Jersey and New York R. R ..... Paterson.

Riverside; village, part of Newark City, Essex County, on Passaic River and on Paterson and Newark Branch of New York, Lake Erie and Western R. R ..... Paterson.

Riverside; town in Delran Township, Burlington County, on Delaware River and on Amboy Division Pennsylvania R. R. ..... Burlington.

Riverton; town in Cinnaminson Township, Burlington County, on Pennsylvania R. R., Amboy Division ..... Germantown.

Rivervale; village in Washington Township, Bergen County, on Hackensack River ..... Ramapo.

Roadstown; village in Hopewell Township, Cumberland County ..... Bayside.

Roaring; brook rising in Hillsboro Township, Somerset County, flowing into Crusers Brook in Montgomery Township ..... Princeton.

Robanna; village in Monroe Township, Gloucester County, on Philadelphia and Reading R. R. ..... Glassboro.

Robbinsville; village in Washington Township, Mercer County, on Pennsylvania R. R., Amboy Division ..... Bordentown.

Roberts Branch; brook in Woodland and Shamong townships, Burlington County, tributary to Batsto River. { Pemberton. { Mullica.

Robertsville; village in Marlboro Township, Monmouth County ..... New Brunswick.

Robinson; beach on coast of Maurice River Township, Cumberland County ..... Dennisville.

Robinson; branch of Rahway River in Union County, flowing into that river at Rahway City ..... Plainfield.

Robinvale; village in Raritan Township, Middlesex County, on Pennsylvania R. R. ..... Plainfield.

Rochelle Park; village in Saddle River Township, Bergen County, on Saddle River and on New York, Susquehanna and Western R. R. ..... Paterson.

Rock; brook in Hillsboro and Montgomery townships, Somerset County, tributary to Bedens Brook. { Princeton. { Lambertville.

Rock; point projecting into Great Egg Harbor, Weymouth Township, Atlantic County ..... Great Egg Harbor.

Rock Mill; village in Hillsboro Township, Somerset County. Princeton.

Rockaway; township in Morris County; area, 63 square miles { Greenwood Lake. { Morristown. { Lake Hopatcong.

Names of sheets.

Rockaway; river in Morris County, flowing into Passaic River. — Franklin. Morristown. Lake Hopatcong.

Rockaway; creek in Hunterdon County, formed by two branches, the North Branch and the South Branch, tributary to Lamington River. — High Bridge. Somerville.

Rockaway; village in Rockaway Township, Morris County, on Rockaway River and on Morris Canal.............. Lake Hopatcong.

Rockaway Valley; village in Rockaway Township, Morris County, on Rockaway River .... Morristown.

Rockport; village in Wantage Township, Sussex County.... Port Jervis.

Rockport; village in Mansfield Township, Warren County, on Morris Canal.. Hackettstown.

Rocktown; village in East Amwell Township, Hunterdon County .... Lambertville.

Rockwood; village in Hammonton Township, Atlantic County .... Mullica.

Rocky; brook rising in Millstone Township, Monmouth County, flowing northwest on boundary between Monroe Township, Middlesex County, and East Windsor Township, Mercer County, into Millstone River. — Cassville. New Brunswick.

Rocky Hill; borough in Montgomery Township, Somerset County, on Millstone River and on Delaware and Raritan Canal .... Princeton.

Roe; pond in Vernon Township, Sussex County.............. Franklin.

Roe; island in swamp in Independence Township, Warren County... Hackettstown.

Rosedale; village in Lawrence Township, Mercer County, on Stony Brook... Princeton.

Roseland; village in Livingston Township, Essex County... Morristown.

Roselle; town in Linden Township, Union County, at junction of Lehigh Valley R. R. with Central R. R. of New Jersey. Plainfield.

Rosemont; village in Delaware Township, Hunterdon County. Lambertville.

Rosenhayn; village in Deerfield Township, Cumberland County, on New Jersey Southern R. R................... Bridgeton.

Roseville; village, part of Newark City, Essex County, on Morris Canal and on Bloomfield Branch of Delaware, Lackawanna and Western R. R .... Paterson.

Roseville; village in Byram Township, Sussex County, on Lubbers Run .... Lake Hopatcong.

Rotten; pond in Franklin Township, Bergen County........ Greenwood Lake.

Round; mountain in Readington Township, Hunterdon County; altitude, 608 feet................................ High Bridge.

Round; valley in Clinton Township, Hunterdon County..... High Bridge.

Round; pond in Wallpack Township, Sussex County .... Wallpack.

Roundabout; creek in Little Egg Harbor Township, Burlington County, flowing into Great Bay..................... Little Egg Harbor.

Rowlands Mills; village in Readington Township, Hunterdon County, on South Branch of Raritan River and on Lehigh Valley R. R.. High Bridge.

Roxbury; township in Morris County; area, 24 square miles. Lake Hopatcong.

Roxbury; village in Harmony Township, Warren County, on Buckhorn Creek .... Delaware Water Gap.

Roxiticus; village in Mendham Township, Morris County, on North Branch of Raritan River.......................... Lake Hopatcong.

Names of sheets.

Roycefield; village in Hillsboro Township, Somerset County, on South Branch of Central R. R. of New Jersey .... Somerville.

Royces Branch; river in Hillsboro Township, Somerset { Somerville. County, tributary to Millstone River. { Princeton.

Rudeville; village in Hardyston Township, Sussex County.. Franklin.

Rulons; village in Woolwich Township, Gloucester County, on West Jersey R. R .... Chester.

Rum; point projecting from Atlantic Ocean into Absecon Inlet, in Galloway Township, Atlantic County.................. Atlantic City.

Rumson; neck of land in Shrewsbury Township, Monmouth County, between Navesink and Shrewsbury rivers ...... Sandy Hook.

Run Creek; passage in coast swamp in Upper Township, Cape May County .... Sea Isle.

Russia; village in Jefferson Township, Morris County....... Franklin.

Rutherford; borough in Bergen County, formerly in Union Township, on Passaic River .... Paterson.

Saddle; river heading in Rockland County, N. Y., flows ⎫ through Bergen County, N. J., into Passaic River at Gar- ⎬ Ramapo. field. ⎭ Paterson.

Saddle River; township in Bergen County; area, 15 square miles .... Paterson.

Saddle River; village in Orvil Township, Bergen County, on Saddle River... Ramapo.

Saint Cloud; village in West Orange Township, Essex County.. Morristown.

Salem; county in southwest part of the State; area, 389 ⎰ square miles.

⎧ Wilmington.
⎪ Smyrna.
⎪ Chester.
⎨ Salem.
⎪ Bayside.
⎪ Glassboro.
⎩ Bridgeton.

Salem; city in Salem County .... Salem.

Salem; village in Union Township, Union County, on Elizabeth River... Staten Island.

Salem; creek rising in Upper Pittsgrove Township, Salem ⎫Salem. County, flows through Salem County into Delaware ⎬Glassboro. River. ⎭

Salt; island in coast swamp in Galloway Township, Atlantic County .... Atlantic City.

Samptown; village in Piscataway Township, Middlesex County, on Bound Brook and on Lehigh Valley R. R..... Plainfield.

Sand; pond in Wantage Township, Sussex County.......... Port Jervis.

Sand; pond in Vernon Township, Sussex County............ Franklin.

Sand; pond in Hardwick Township, Warren County .... Wallpack.

Sand Brook; village in Delaware Township, Hunterdon County .... Lambertville.

Sand Hills; village in South Brunswick Township, Middlesex County .... Princeton.

Sand Hills; village in Raritan Township, Middlesex County. Plainfield.

Sand Hills; village in Vernon Township, Sussex County.... Franklin.

Sandtown; village in Southampton Township, Burlington County, on Little Creek.................................. Mount Holly.

Sandy; island in Union Township, Ocean County, in Barnegat Bay .... Long Beach.

Names of sheets.

Sandy; ridge in marsh in Shamong Township, Burlington County... Pemberton.
Sandy Hook; bay west of Sandy Hook .... Sandy Hook.
Sandy Hook; northern point of reef on coast of New Jersey. Sandy Hook.
Sandy Hook; life-saving station on Sandy Hook............. Sandy Hook.
Sandy Hook; pier on west side of Sandy Hook............. Sandy Hook.
Sandy Hook; light on west side of Sandy Hook............. Sandy Hook.
Sandyston; township in Sussex County; area, 43 square miles. { Milford, Wallpack. Franklin.
Sarah Run; brook in Stow Creek Township, Cumberland County, flowing into Horse Run .... Bayside.
Sarepta; village in Oxford Township, Warren County, on Beaver Brook... Delaware Water Gap.
Savage; pond in Dennis Township, Cape May County....... Dennisville.
Saw Mill; creek on boundary between Union Township, Bergen County, and Kearney Township, Hudson County, tributary to Hackensack River............................... Paterson.
Saxton Falls; village in Allamuchy Township, Warren County, on Morris Canal and on Musconetcong River.... Hackettstown.
Sayres Neck; peninsula of dry land in coast swamp in Lawrence Township, Cumberland County...................... Bridgeton.
Sayreville; township in Middlesex County; area, 17 square miles .... New Brunswick.
Sayreville; village in Sayreville Township, Middlesex County, on Raritan River................................. New Brunswick.
Schooleys Mountain; village in Washington Township, Morris County... Hackettstown.
Schooner; creek in Upper Township, Cape May County, flowing into Tuckahoe River .... Great Egg Harbor.
Schuetzen Park; village in North Bergen Township, Hudson County, on Northern R. R. of New Jersey and on New York, Susquehanna and Western R. R......... .... Paterson.
Schuyler Corner; village in Union Township, Bergen County. Paterson.
Schraalenburg; village in Palisade Township, Bergen County, on West Shore R. R................................... Harlem.
Scobeyville; village in Atlantic Township, Monmouth County .... Sandy Hook.
Scotch Bonnet; passage in coast swamp in Middle Township, Cape May County................................. Dennisville.
Scotch Plains; village in Fanwood Township, Union County, on Green Brook.. Plainfield.
Scotland Run; brook running southwest through Gloucester County into Maurice River.............................. Glassboro.
Scott; mountain in Warren County; is a part of South Mountain. { Easton. Delaware Water Gap.
Scott Corner; village in South Brunswick Township, Middlesex County .... Princeton.
Scull; landing in Egg Harbor Township, Atlantic County, on Egg Harbor River .... Great Egg Harbor.
Scull; bay in coast swamp in Egg Harbor Township, Atlantic County... Great Egg Harbor.
Sea Breeze; village on coast of Fairfield Township, Cumberland County.. Bayside.

Names of sheets.

Sea Girt; village in Wall Township, Monmouth County, on New York and Long Branch R. R.......................... Asbury Park.

Sea Girt; inlet, extending from Atlantic Ocean into Wall Township, Monmouth County............................. Asbury Park.

Sea Haven; village on coast of Little Egg Harbor Township, Burlington County... Little Egg Harbor.

Sea Isle City; borough on coast of Cape May County....... Sea Isle.

Sea Isle City; life-saving station on northeast coast of Dennis Township, Cape May County.......................... Sea Isle.

Sea Isle Junction; village in northern part of Dennis Township, Cape May County.................................... Dennisville.

Sea Plain; village in Wall Township, Monmouth County, on New York and Long Branch R. R.......................... Asbury Park.

Seabright; village in Shrewsbury Township, Monmouth County... Sandy Hook.

Seabright; life-saving station on reef in Shrewsbury Township, Monmouth County..................................... Sandy Hook.

Seaside Park; village on reef in Berkeley Township, Ocean County, on Philadelphia and Long Branch R. R........... Barnegat.

Seaview; village in southern part of Egg Harbor Township, Atlantic County... Great Egg Harbor

Seaville; village in southeast part Upper Township, Cape May County... Sea Isle.

Seaweed; point projecting from Metedeconk Neck into Barnegat Bay, in Brick Township, Ocean County........... Asbury Park.

Secaucus; village in central part North Bergen Township, Hudson County... Paterson.

Second; river in eastern part Essex County, flows into Passaic River... Paterson.

Second Branch; brook in Mullica Township, Atlantic County Mullica.

Second Watchung; mountain ridge extending parallel with First Watchung Mountain through Passaic, Essex, Union, and Somerset counties. { Paterson. / Morristown. / Somerset. / Plainfield.

Sedge; group of islands in Barnegat Bay, in Ocean Township, Ocean County... Barnegat.

Sergeantsville; village in central part Delaware Township, Hunterdon County....................................... Lambertville.

Seven; group of islands in Great Bay, in Little Egg Harbor Township, Burlington County............................ Little Egg Harbor.

Seven Mile; beach along southeast shore of Middle Township, Cape May County. { Sea Isle. / Dennisville.

Seven Stars; village in Brick Township, Ocean County..... Asbury Park.

Sewaren; village in Woodbridge Township, Middlesex County, on Arthur Kill and on New York and Long Branch R. R.. Plainfield.

Sewell; village in Mantua Township, Gloucester County, on West Jersey R. R.. Philadelphia.

Sewell; point extending from southeast part of Lower Township, Cape May County, into Atlantic Ocean.............. Cape May.

Shabakunk; creek in Mercer County...................... { Lambertville. / Princeton.

Shad; island in Little Bay, Galloway Township, Atlantic County... Atlantic City.

Shady Side; village in southeastern part Ridgefield Township, Bergen County, on Hudson River................... Harlem.

Names of sheets.

Shamong; township in Burlington County; area, 70 square miles. ⎰ Pemberton. ⎱ Hammonton. ⎰ Mount Holly. ⎱ Mullica.

Shane Branch; brook in Burlington County .... Pemberton.

Shannoc; brook in Jackson Township, Ocean County .... Cassville.

Shark River; village in Neptune Township, Monmouth County, on Shark River .... Asbury Park.

Shark River; village in Wall Township, Monmouth County, on New Jersey Southern R. R .... Asbury Park.

Shark River; inlet extending from Atlantic Ocean into Monmouth County .... Asbury Park.

Shark River; life-saving station on coast of Neptune Township, Monmouth County .... Asbury Park.

Sharon; village in Upper Freehold Township, Monmouth County .... Bordentown.

Sharp Branch; brook in east part of Maurice River Township, Cumberland County; flows east into Tuckahoe River ... Tuckahoe.

Sharp Rook; an indentation of Lake Hopatcong into the eastern coast of Byram Township, Sussex County .... Lake Hopatcong.

Sharp Run; brook in Evesham and Medford townships, Burlington County .... Mount Holly

Sharptown; village in Pilesgrove Township, Salem County. Salem.

Shaw Branch; brook in Hopewell Township, Cumberland County. ⎰ Bayside, ⎱ Bridgeton.

Sheepshead; passage in coast swamp in Little Egg Harbor Township, Burlington County............................. Little Egg Harbor.

Shell; landing in Middle Township, Cape May County ...... Dennisville.

Shelter; island in Little Egg Harbor, in Eagleswood Township, Ocean County .... Little Egg Harbor.

Shelter Islands; bay in coast swamp in Egg Harbor Township, Atlantic County .... Great Egg Harbor.

Sheppard; pond in northeastern part of Pompton Township, Passaic County, N. J., extending into Rockland County, N. Y.. Ramapo.

Sheppard Mill; village in Greenwich Township, Cumberland County, on New Jersey Southern R. R .... Bayside.

· **Shiloh**; village in Stowe Creek Township, Cumberland County. Bayside

Shiloh; village in eastern part of Hope Township, and partly in Frelinghuysen Township, Warren County............ Hackettstown.

Shinn Branch; brook in Woodland Township, Burlington County .... Pemberton.

Shipetaukin; creek in Lawrence Township, Mercer County. Princeton.

Shippenport; village in northwestern part of Roxbury Township, Morris County, on Morris Canal and on Delaware, Lackawanna and Western R. R........................... Lake Hopatcong.

Ships Bottom; life-saving station on coast of Stafford Township, Ocean County................................. Long Beach.

Shirley; village in Upper Pittsgrove Township, Salem County .... Glassboro.

Shoal Branch: brook in Woodland and Randolph townships, Burlington County. ⎰ Whitings. ⎱ Pemberton. ⎱ Mullica.

108   A GEOGRAPHIC DICTIONARY OF NEW JERSEY.

Names of sheets.

Shongum; village in eastern part Randolph Township, Morris County .... Lake Hopatcong.

Shooting Thorofare; passage in coast swamp in Little Harbor Township, Burlington County .... Little Egg Harbor.

Shord Mill; brook in Little Egg Harbor Township, Burlington County, tributary to Turkerton Creek................. Little Egg Harbor.

Short Hills; village in Millburn Township, Essex County, on Delaware, Lackawanna and Western R. R........... Plainfield.

Shreve Branch; brook in Woodland Township, Burlington County, tributary to Shoal Branch .... Whitings.

Shrewsbury; township in Monmouth County; area, 33 square miles. — Sandy Hook. / Asbury Park.

Shrewsbury; village in Shrewsbury Township, Monmouth County, on New Jersey Southern R. R..................... Sandy Hook.

Shrewsbury; river in Monmouth County, flows into Sandy Hook Bay .... Sandy Hook.

Shuster; pond in eastern part Hardwick Township, Warren County .... Wallpack.

Sicklerville; village in Winslow Township, Camden County, on Philadelphia and Reading R. R .... Hammonton

Sicomac; village in southern part of Franklin Township, Bergen County .... Paterson.

Sidney; village in northern part Franklin Township, Hunterdon County... High Bridge.

Signey; run in Gloucester Township, Camden County....... Philadelphia.

Siloam; village in Freehold Township, Monmouth County .. Cassville.

Silver; lake in northeastern part of Hope Township, Warren County .... Hackettstown.

Silver Lake; village in Belleville Township, Essex County, Morris Canal .... Paterson.

Silver Run; brook in Millville Township, Cumberland County; flows into Maurice River .... Bridgeton.

Silverton; village in Dover Township, Ocean County....... Asbury Park.

Simkin Thorofare; passage in coast swamp in Galloway Township, Atlantic County................................. Atlantic City.

Simonson; brook in Franklin Township, Somerset County; flows into Millstone River at Griggstown .... Princeton.

Singac; village in western part of Little Falls Township, Passaic County, on Passaic River and on New York and Greenwood Lake R. R..................................... Paterson

Six Mile Run; river rising in North Brunswick Township, Middlesex County; flows west and empties into Millstone River in Franklin Township, Somerset County. — Somerset. / New Brunswick.

Six Points; village in Pittsgrove Township, Salem County.. Glassboro

Skillman; village in western part Montgomery Township, Somerset County, on Philadelphia and Reading R. R.... Princeton.

Skit Branch; brook in Shamong Township, Burlington County .... Pemberton.

Skunk; sound in southern part of Lower Township, Cape May County .... Cape May.

Slab Branch; small brook in Maurice River Township, Cumberland County, tributary to Muskee Creek .... Tuckahoe.

Slab Causeway Branch; brook in Woodland Township, Burlington County, tributary to Burrs Mill Brook....... Pemberton.

Names of sheets.

Sledge; creek in southeastern part Weymouth Township, Atlantic County, flows north into Middle River........... Great Egg Harbor.

Sloop ; point projecting from Metedeconk Neck, in Brick Township, Ocean County, in Barnegat Bay................ Asbury Park.

Sloop Sedge; island in Barnegat Bay in Union Township, Ocean County .... Long Beach

Sloop Thorofare; passage in coast swamp in Galloway Township, Atlantic County.................................... Atlantic County.

Slough; brook in Livingston Township, Essex County, tributary to Passaic River... Morristown.

Sluice; creek rising in northeastern part Middle Township, Cape May County, flowing northwest into Dennis Creek.. Dennisville.

Small; village in Shamong Township, Burlington County.... Mount Holly.

Smith; landing in Egg Harbor Township, Atlantic County, on Lake Bay... Great Egg Harbor.

Smith; creek in Woodbridge Township, Middlesex County, tributary to Arthur Kill. { Staten Island. { Plainfield.

Smith ; ferry on southwest coast of Wallpack Township, Sussex County, on Delaware River......................... Wallpack.

Smith Mills; village in southeastern part of West Milford Township in Passaic County, on Pequannock River, and on New York, Susquehanna and Western R. R............. Greenwood Lake.

Smithburg; village in Freehold Township, Monmouth County .... Cassville.

Smithville; village in Easthampton Township, Burlington County, on Rancocas Creek. { Pemberton. { Mount Holly.

Smithville; village in Galloway Township, Atlantic County. Atlantic City.

Snake; hill in southwestern part of North Bergen Township, Hudson County; altitude, 203 feet .... Paterson.

Snow Hill; village in eastern part Center Township, Camden County... Philadelphia.

Syndertown; village in southwestern part of East Amwell Township, Hunterdon County .... Lambertville.

Sod Thorofare; passage in coast swamp in Egg Harbor Township, Atlantic County .... Great Egg Harbor.

Soho; village in Belleville Township, Essex County, on Second River and on New York and Greenwood Lake R. R. Paterson.

Somers Point; borough in Egg Harbor Township, Atlantic County... Great Egg Harbor.

Somers; cove projecting from Reed Bay in Galloway Township, Atlantic County..................................... Atlantic City.

Somerset; county in central part of State; area, 305 square miles. { High Bridge. { Lambertville. { Princeton. { Somerville. { Plainfield. { New Brunswick.

Somerset; village in western part Ewing Township, Mercer County, on Delaware River, on Delaware and Raritan Canal, and on Belvidere Division Pennsylvania R. R..... Lambertville.

Somerville; village in central part of Galloway Township, Atlantic County .... Atlantic City.

Somerville; borough in southern part of Bridgewater Township, Somerset County, on Raritan River, at junction of South Branch R. R. with Central R. R. of New Jersey... Somerville.

Names of sheets.

Somerville Station; village in Gloucester Township, Camden County, on Philadelphia and Reading R. R. (Atlantic City Line) .... Philadelphia.

Sooy Place; village in Woodland Township, Burlington County... Pemberton.

South; hill in Shrewsbury Township, Monmouth County; elevation, 161 feet .... Sandy Hook

South; river rising in northern part of Buena Vista Township; flows southeast through Hamilton Township, forming partial boundary between it and Weymouth Township, into Great Egg Harbor River, Atlantic County ..... Great Egg Harbor.

South; branch of Rahway River, in Middlesex County, and enters that river at Rahway City.......................... Plainfield.

South; river forming boundary between Sayreville and East Brunswick townships, Middlesex County; flows into Raritan River... New Brunswick.

South; beacon on Sandy Hook................................. Sandy Hook.

South Amboy; township in Middlesex County; area, 1 square mile... New Brunswick.

South Amboy; village in Sayreville Township, Middlesex County, on Camden and Amboy R. R., and on New York and Long Branch R. R .... New Brunswick.

South Atlantic City; borough on coast of Egg Harbor Township, Atlantic County.. Atlantic City.

South Branch; village in northwestern part Hillsboro Township, Somerset County, on South Branch of Raritan River.. Somerville.

South Branch; brook in Woodland Township, Burlington County, tributary to Burrs Mill Brook .... Pemberton,

South Branch; brook in South Harrison and Harrison townships, Gloucester County, tributary to Raccoon Creek. } Glassboro. Salem.

South Brigantine; life-saving station on Brigantine Beach.. Atlantic City.

South Brunswick; township in Middlesex County; area, 49 square miles. } Princeton. New Brunswick.

South Channel; passage in coast swamp in Middle Township, Cape May County .... Sea Isle.

South Dennisville; village in southern central part Dennis Township, Cape May County............................... Dennisville.

South Harrison; township in Gloucester County; area, 20 square miles .... } Glassboro. Salem.

South Orange; township in Essex County; area, 8 square miles. } Morristown. Plainfield. Paterson. Staten Island.

South Orange; borough in central part South Orange Township, Essex County, on Delaware, Lackawanna and Western R. R.. Plainfield.

South Plainfield; village in northeastern part of Piscataway Township, Middlesex County, on Bound Brook and on Lehigh Valley R. R.. Plainfield.

South Run; brook in New Hanover, Burlington County, and Plumstead Township, Ocean County, tributary to Crosswick Creek. } Bordentown. Cassville.

Names of sheets.

South Seaville; village in eastern part of Dennis Township, Cape May County.. Dennisville.

South Somerville; village in northern part Hillsboro Township, Somerset County, on Lehigh Valley R. R .... Somerville.

South Vineland; village in Landis Township, Cumberland County, on West Jersey R. R............................ Bridgeton.

Southampton; township in Burlington County; area, 47 square miles. { Pemberton. { Mount Holly.

Southtown; village in southern part of Frelinghuysen Township, Warren County................................ Hackettstown.

Sow and Pigs; creek in Downe Township, Cumberland County, flows into Delaware River .... Bridgeton.

Spa Spring; village in Perth Amboy Township, Middlesex County .... Plainfield.

Sparta; township in Sussex County; area, 42 square miles.. { Franklin. { Lake Hopatcong.

Sparta; village in central part of Sparta Township, Sussex County .... Franklin.

Sparta; mountain in Byram Township, Sussex County...... Lake Hopatcong.

Sparta Junction; village in western part of Sparta Township, Sussex County.. Franklin.

Sparta Station; village in northwestern part Sparta Township, on Sussex R. R., Sussex County..................... Franklin.

Speedwell; village in Woodland Township, Burlington County .... Pemberton.

Spermaceti; cove in west shore Sandy Hook............... Sandy Hook.

Spermaceti Cove, life-saving station on Sandy Hook....... Sandy Hook.

Spicertown; village in southwestern part of Rockaway Township, Morris County.. Lake Hopatcong.

Splitrock; village in eastern part of Rockaway Township, Morris County .... Morristown.

Splitrock; pond in the northeastern part of Rockaway Township, Morris County .... Morristown.

Spotswood; village in East Brunswick Township, Middlesex County, on Camden and Amboy R. R .... New Brunswick.

Spraguetown; village in Eagleswood Township, Ocean County, on Westecunk Creek............................... Little Egg Harbor.

Spring; lake in Wall Township, Monmouth County.......... Asbury Park.

Spring Hill; group of four hills in Woodland and Randolph townships, Burlington County; elevation, 168, 168, 174, and 176 feet, respectively................................ Whitings.

Spring Lake; village in Wall Township, Monmouth County. Asbury Park.

Spring Lake; life-saving station on coast of Wall Township, Monmouth County.. Asbury Park.

Spring Mills; village in Gloucester Township, Camden County Philadelphia.

Spring Mills; village in central part of Holland Township, Hunterdon County.. Easton.

Spring Valley; village in central part of Midland Township, Bergen County .... Paterson.

Springdale; village in Delaware Township, Camden County, on Philadelphia, Marlton and Medford R. R .... Mount Holly.

Springdale; village in western part of Andover Township, Sussex County, on Pequest River...................... Wallpack River

Springer; creek in Shamong Township, Burlington County, flows into Batsto River. { Mullica. { Mount Holly. { Pemberton.

112   A GEOGRAPHIC DICTIONARY OF NEW JERSEY.

Names of sheets.

Springfield; township in Union County; area, 5 square miles. Plainfield.

Springfield; township in Burlington County; area, 30 square miles. { Bordentown. Burlington. Pemberton.

Springfield; village in Springfield Township, Burlington County .... Bordentown.

Springfield; town coextensive with Springfield Township, Union County .... Plainfield.

Springtown; village in Greenwich Township, Cumberland County .... Bayside.

Springtown; village in central part of Washington Township, Morris County .... Hackettstown.

Springtown; village in central part of Pohatcong Township, Warren County .... Easton.

Sprout; brook in Midland Township, Bergen County, tributary to Saddle River .... Paterson.

Spruce Run; brook rising in northern part of Lebanon Township, Hunterdon County, enters South Branch of Raritan River at Clinton .... High Bridge.

Squan Beach; life-saving station on coast of Wall Township, Monmouth County .... Asbury Park.

Squankum; village in Howell Township, Monmouth County. Asbury Park.

Squankum; brook in Howell Township, Monmouth County, flows into Manasquan River .... Asbury Park.

Squankum Branch; brook in Monroe Township, Gloucester County, flows into Great Egg Harbor River .... Hammonton.

Stafford; township in Ocean County; area, 56 square miles. { Whitings. Little Egg Harbor. Long Beach.

Stafford Forge; village in Eagleswood Township, Ocean County .... Little Egg Harbor.

Staffordville; village in Eagleswood Township, Ocean County, on Tuckerton R. R .... Little Egg Harbor.

Stag; pond in northern part of Byram Township, Sussex County .... Lake Hopatcong.

Stanhope; village in southern part of Byram Township, Sussex County, extending on over the boundary into Mount Olive Township, Morris County, on Morris Canal and on Delaware, Lackawanna and Western R. R .... Lake Hopatcong.

Stanley; village in northern part of Summit Township, Union County, on Passaic River .... Plainfield.

Stanton; village in southwestern part of Readington Township, Hunterdon County .... High Bridge.

Stanton Station; village in southwestern part of Readington Township, Hunterdon County, on South Branch of Raritan River and on Lehigh Valley R. R .... High Bridge.

Star Landing; village in eastern part of Woodbridge Township, Middlesex County, on Arthur Kill .... Staten Island.

Starrs Station; part of Camden City, on Camden and Atlantic R. R .... Philadelphia.

Staten Island; called Arthur Kill and Kill van Kull; sound separating Staten Island from Middlesex and Union counties, and extending from Raritan Bay to Newark Bay and New York Upper Bay. { Plainfield. Staten Island.

Names of sheets.

Stathem; neck of land between Newport and Phillips creeks, in Greenwich Township, Cumberland County........... Bayside.

Station; village in northern part of Harmony Township, Warren County, on Delaware River and Belvidere Division of Pennsylvania R. R..... .... Delaware Water Gap.

Steelman; bay in coast swamp in Galloway Township, Atlantic County... Atlantic City.

Steelman; bay in coast swamp in Egg Harbor Township, Atlantic County, flows into Great Egg Harbor............. Great Egg Harbor.

Steelman; landing in Weymouth Township, Atlantic County, on Great Egg Harbor River.............................. Great Egg Harbor.

Steelman Thorofare; passage in coast swamp in Galloway Township, Atlantic County............................ Atlantic City.

Steelmansville; village in southern part of Egg Harbor Township, Atlantic County............................ Great Egg Harbor.

Steelmantown; village in southern part Upper Township, Cape May County... Tuckahoe.

Steep Run; brook in Commercial Township, Cumberland County, flows into Maurice River....................... Bridgeton.

Stelton; village in southwestern part of Raritan Township, Middlesex County, on Pennsylvania R. R.............. Plainfield.

Stephens; creek rising in northwestern part of Weymouth Township, Atlantic County, flows southeast into Great Egg Harbor River. } Tuckahoe. Great Egg Harbor.

Stephens; brook in eastern part of Roxbury Township, flowing into Morris Canal and tributary to Rockaway River. Lake Hopatcong.

Stephensburg; village in western part of Washington Township, Morris County.................................. Hackettstown.

Stewartsville; town in northern part of Greenwich Township, Warren County, on Morris Canal and on the Delaware, Lackawanna, and Western R. R..................... Easton.

Stickle; pond in western part of Andover Township, Sussex County...................................... Wallpack.

Stickle; pond in western part of Pequannock Township, Morris County.................................... Morristown.

Still House; brook in Manalapan Township, Monmouth County, flowing into Manalapan brook.................... New Brunswick.

Still Run; brook in Greenwich Township, Gloucester County, tributary to Ramapo Creek.................... Chester.

Still Run; brook in Glassboro, Clayton, and Franklin Townships, Gloucester County, flows into Maurice River...... Glassboro.

Still Valley; village in western part of Greenwich Township, Warren County... Easton.

Stillwater; township in Sussex County; area, 38 square miles. } Hackettstown. Wallpack.

Stillwater; village in southwestern part of Stillwater Township, Sussex County, on Paulins Kill..................... Wallpack.

Stipson; islands in swamp in southwestern part of Dennis Township, Cape May County.............................. Dennisville.

Stirling; village in eastern part of Passaic Township, Morris County, on Passaic and Delaware R. R.................. Plainfield.

Stites; sound in northeastern part of Middle Township, Cape May County. } Dennisville. Sea Isle.

Names of sheets.

Stockholm; village in southeastern part of Hardyston Township, on New York, Susquehanna, and Western R. R., in Sussex County... Franklin.

Stockton; township in Camden County; area, 15 square miles Philadelphia.

Stockton; village in Stockton Township, Camden County, on Pennsylvania R. R....................................... Philadelphia.

Stockton; village in southern part of Delaware Township, Hunterdon County, on Delaware River.................... Lambertville.

Stone; hill in Atlantic Township, Monmouth County; elevation, 194 feet.. Sandy Hook.

Stone Bridge Run; brook in Deerfield and Bridgeton Townships, Cumberland County, flows into Cohansey Creek... Bridgetown.

Stone Hollow Branch; brook in Stafford Township, Ocean County, flows into Mill Creek............................. Little Egg Harbor.

Stone House; brook in Pequannock Township, Morris { Greenwood Lake.
County, tributary to Pequannock River. { Morristown.

Stonetown; village in western part of Pompton Township, Passaic County... Greenwood Lake.

Stony; brook rises in Hunterdon County, flows east through }
Mercer County, and empties into Millstone River after { Lambertville.
forming boundary between Princeton and West Windsor { Princeton.
Townships. }

Stony; brook rising in Pequannock Township, flows southwest through Montville Township and Boonville Township, emptying into Rockaway River in southeastern part of Rockaway Township, Morris County .... Morristown.

Stony; brook in Washington Township, Morris County, tributary to South Branch Raritan River..................... Hackettstown.

Stony; brook, rises in Warren Township, flows across South Plainfield Township, and empties into Green Brook, in Somerset County .... Plainfield.

Stony; inlet projecting from Delaware River into Lower Alloways Creek Township, Salem County................... Bayside.

Stop-the-jade; brook in Southampton Township, on boundary between that and Pemberton townships, Burlington } Mount Holly.
County, flows into South Branch of Rancocas Creek. { Pemberton.

Stormy; hill in Randolph Township, Burlington County; elevation, 72 feet.. Mullica.

Story; island in Little Egg Harbor, in Little Egg Harbor Township, Burlington County............................. Little Egg Harbor.

Stout; creek in Lacey Township, Ocean County, flows in Barnegat Bay... Barnegat.

Stoutsburg; village in western part of Montgomery Township, Somerset County .... Princeton.

Stow; creek heading in Lower Alloways Creek Township, Salem County, flows south, forming boundary between Stow Creek and Greenwich townships, Cumberland County, and Lower Alloways Creek Township, into Delaware River... Bayside.

Stow Creek; township in Cumberland County; area, 19 { Bayside.
square miles. { Salem.

Straight; creek (passage) in coast swamp in Downe Township, Cumberland County .... Maurice River.

Names of sheets.

Stretche Run; brook in Lower Alloways Creek Township, Salem County, and Hopewell Township, Cumberland County, flows into Cohansey Creek. } Bridgeton. Salem.

Styx River; an arm of Lake Hopatcong indenting the eastern coast of Byram Township, Sussex County .... Lake Hopatcong.

Succasunna; village in southeastern part of Roxbury Township, Morris County, on Chester branch of Delaware, Lackawanna and Western R. R .... Lake Hopatcong.

Success; village in Jackson Township, Ocean County...... Cassville.

Sucker; pond in western part of Stillwater Township, Sussex County .... Wallpack.

Sugarloaf; hill in Atlantic Township, Monmouth County; elevation, 199 feet.. Sandy Hook.

Summerfield; village in southern part of Oxford Township, Warren County.. Delaware Water Gap.

Summit; township in Union County; area, 6 square miles .. Plainfield.

Summit; village in Summit Township, Union County, on Delaware, Lackawanna and Western R. R .... Plainfield.

Sunfish; pond in Pahaquarry Township, Warren County.... Bushkill Falls.

Sunken Branch; brook forming partial boundary between Dover and Berkeley townships; tributary to Toms River. Barnegat.

Sunset; lake in Ocean Township, Monmouth County........ Asbury Park.

Sussex; county in extreme northern part of State; area, 535 square miles. { Hackettstown. Lake Hopatcong. Wallpack. Milford. Port Jervis. Franklin. Goshen. Greenwood Lake.

Sussex Mills; village in western part of Sparta Township, Sussex County .... Franklin.

Swain; railroad station in north central part of Middle Township, Cape May County, on West Jersey R. R....... Dennisville.

Swan; point projecting from Metedeconk Neck, in Brick Township, Ocean County, into Barnegat Bay .... Asbury Park.

Swan; pond in southeastern part of Weymouth Township, Atlantic County .... Great Egg Harbor.

Swan; bay; an enlargement of Mullica River, in Bass River Township, Burlington County .... Little Egg Harbor.

Swann; channel in southeastern part of Lower Township; tributary to Grassy Sound................................ Cape May.

Swartswood; village in eastern part of Stillwater Township, Sussex County, on Swartswood Lake................ Wallpack.

Swartswood; lake in eastern part of Stillwater Township, Sussex County.. Wallpack.

Swartswood Station; village in western part of Hampton Township, Sussex County, on Paulins Kill and on New York, Susquehanna and Western R. R.................... Wallpack.

Swayzes Mills; village in western part of Hope Township, Warren County, on Muddy Brook........................ Hackettstown.

Swede Run; brook in Mannington Township, Salem County, flows into Mannington Creek................................ Salem.

Names of sheets.

Swede Run; brook in Chester and Delran townships, Burlington County, flows into Delaware River. { Burlington. Mount Holly.

Swedesboro; town in Gloucester County, on West Jersey R. R.. Salem.

Sweeten Water; small brook in northwestern part Maurice River Township, Cumberland County, flows into Manumuskin River.. Tuckahoe.

Swimming; river heading in three branches; forms partial boundary between Middletown and Shrewsbury townships, Monmouth County; flows into Navesink River.... Sandy Hook.

Swimming; creek in northeastern part of Dennis Township, Cape May County, flowing into Ludlam Bay.............. Sea Isle.

Swinefield Bridge; village in southeastern part of Hanover Township, Morris County, on Passaic River.............. Morristown.

Swinesburg; village in northern part of Alexandria Township, Hunterdon County .... Easton.

Sykes Branch; brook in Woodland Township, Burlington County, tributary to Shoal Branch .... Whitings.

Sykesville; village in New Hanover Township, Burlington County.. Bordentown.

Tabernacle; village in Shamong Township, Burlington County .... Pemberton.

Tabor; village in northwestern part of Hanover Township, Morris County, on Delaware, Lackawanna and Western R. R... Morristown.

Tammany; hill in northwestern part of Knowlton extending into Pahaquarry Township, Warren County; altitude, 1,600 feet.. Delaware Water Gap.

Tanners; brook, tributary to Black River, in Washington and Chester townships, Morris County. { Lake Hopatcong. Hackettstown.

Tarkiln Branch; brook in Landis Township, Cumberland County, flows into Parvin Branch of Maurice River...... Bridgeton.

Tarkiln; brook heading in Maurice River Township, Cumberland County, flows northeast across Upper Township, Cape May County, into Tuckahoe River................... Tuckahoe.

Tarkiln; brook in Brick Township, Ocean County, tributary to Kettle Creek .... Asbury Park.

Tatems; village in West Deptford Township, Gloucester County, on West Jersey R. R............................. Philadelphia.

Tatham; life-saving station on east coast Middle Township, Cape May County... Sea Isle.

Taunton; village in Evesham Township, Burlington County. Mount Holly.

Taylortown; village in northwestern part Montville Township, Morris County...................................... Morristown.

Taylorville; village in northeastern part Ridgefield Township, Bergen County .... Harlem.

Tea Neck; village in southern part of Englewood Township, Bergen County.................................... Paterson.

Telegraph; hill in Middletown Township, Monmouth County; elevation 252 feet .... Sandy Hook.

Ten Mile Hollow; valley in Lacey and Berkeley townships, Ocean County .... Whitings.

Ten Mile Run; river rises in south Brunswick Township, Middlesex County, and flows into Millstone River, in Franklin Township, Somerset County .... Princeton.

Names of sheets.

Ten Mile Run; village in Franklin Township, Somerset County .... Princeton.

Tenafly; town in eastern part of Palisade Township, Bergen County, on Tienekill Creek and on Northern R. R. of New Jersey .... Harlem.

Tennent; brook in Madison Township, Middlesex County; flows into Smith River .... New Brunswick.

Tennent; village in Manalapan Township, Monmouth County, on Freehold and Jamesburg R. R .... New Brunswick.

Tepehemus; brook in Marlboro and Manalapan townships, Monmouth County, flows into McGellaird Brook .... New Brunswick.

Terhunes; run in South Brunswick Township, Middlesex County, tributary to Lawrence Brook .... Princeton.

Terrace; pond in western part of West Milford Township, Passaic County .... Greenwood Lake.

Terrapin Gut; brook in Lower Alloways Creek Township, Salem County, flows into Mad Horse Run .... Bayside.

Tewksbury; township in Hunterdon County, area 32 square) High Bridge.
miles. (Somerville.

Texas; village in Monroe Township, Middlesex County, on Matchaponix Brook .... New Brunswick.

Three Bridges; village in southern part Reading Township, Hunterdon County, on South Branch of Raritan River, on Lehigh Valley R. R., and South Branch Central R. R. of New Jersey .... High Bridge.

Three Tuns; village in Mansfield Township, Burlington County .... Bordentown.

Thompsons; point projecting from Greenwich Township, Gloucester County, into the Delaware River .... Chester.

Thompsontown; village in Hamilton Township, Atlantic County, on Great Egg Harbor River .... Great Egg Harbor.

Thorofare; island in Manahawken Bay, in Stafford Township, Ocean County .... Long Beach.

Thorofare; village in West Deptford Township, Gloucester County, on Delaware River R .... Philadelphia.

Tibbs Branch; brook in Woodland Township, Burlington County, flows into Gates Branch .... Pemberton.

Tices; pond in eastern part of Pompton Township, Passaic County .... Greenwood Lake.

Tienekill; creek in Harrington and Palisade townships, Bergen County, tributary to Hackensack River .... Harlem.

Tilton; point on coast of Dover Township, Ocean County.... Barnegat.

Tindale; run in Delaware Township, Camden County, tributary to Coopers Creek .... Philadelphia.

Tindall; island in coast swamp in Greenwich Township, Cumberland County .... Bayside.

Tindell; landing in Fairfield Township, Cumberland County, on Cohansey Creek .... Bridgeton.

Tinton Falls; village in Shrewsbury Township, Monmouth County, on Pine Brook .... Sandy Hook.

Timber; small brook in northern part of Rockaway Township, Morris County; tributary to Pequannock River .... Greenwood Lake.

Timber and Beaver; swamp in northeastern part of Middle Township and southeastern part of Dennis Township, Cape May County .... Dennisville.

118   A GEOGRAPHIC DICTIONARY OF NEW JERSEY.

Names of sheets.

Timber Run; brook in Monroe Township, Middlesex County, flows into Rock Brook ..... New Brunswick.

Timbuctoo; village in West Hampton Township, Burlington County ..... Burlington.

Titusville; village in western part of Hopewell Township, Mercer County, on Delaware River and Pennsylvania R. R., Belvidere division, and on Delaware and Raritan Canal.. Lambertsville.

Tomlins; village in Greenwich Township, Gloucester County, on West Jersey R. R ..... Chester.

Toms; river forming boundary between Dover and Berkeley townships, Ocean County; flows into Barnegat Bay. { Cassville, Asbury Park, Barnegat.

Toms Point; hill in southeastern part of Pequannock Township, Morris County; altitude, 223 feet..... Morristown.

Toms River; life-saving station on reef in Berkeley Township, Ocean County..... Barnegat.

Toms River; village in Dover Township, Ocean County, on Toms River..... Barnegat.

Toneys; brook in Montclair and Bloomfield townships, Essex County; tributary to Second River..... Paterson.

Totowa; village in southwestern part of Manchester Township, Passaic County..... Paterson.

Town Bank; beach on western coast of Lower Township, Cape May County..... Cape May.

Town Neck; creek in Shrewsbury Township, Monmouth County; flows into Shrewsbury River..... Sandy Hook.

Townsbury; village in southern part of Hope Township, Warren County, on Pequest River, and on Lehigh and Hudson River R. R..... Hackettstown.

Townsend; inlet extending from Atlantic Ocean into northeastern coast Middle Township, Cape May County. { Dennisville. Sea Isle.

Townsend; sound in southeastern part of Dennis Township, Cape May County..... Sea Isle.

Townsend Inlet; life-saving station at boundary between Dennis and Middle townships, on coast of Cape May county..... Sea Isle.

Townsend Inlet; village in central part of Middle Township, Cape May County..... Dennisville.

Tracey; village in Monroe Township, Middlesex County, on Freehold and Jamesburg R. R..... New Brunswick.

Tranquility; village in southern part of Green Township, Sussex County, on Lehigh and Hudson River R. R..... Hackettstown.

Tremley; village in southeastern part of Linden Township, Union County, on New York and Long Branch R. R..... Staten Island.

Trenton; city, capital of the State, in Mercer County; area, 3 square miles. { Bordentown, Burlington.

Trenton Junction; village in Ewing Township, Mercer County, at junction of Trenton Branch with New York division of Philadelphia and Reading R. R..... Lambertville.

Troy; brook in Hanover Township, Morris County; tributary to Whippany River..... Morristown.

Troy; meadows in eastern part of Hanover Township, Morris County..... Morristown.

Troy Hills; village in central part of Hanover Township, Morris County, on Troy Brook..... Morristown.

Names of sheets.

Trout; brook rising in Frelinghuysen Township, Warren County; flows southwest and empties into Beaver Brook, in northern part of Hope Township....................... Hackettstown.

Trout; brook in Stillwater Township, Sussex County; tributary to Paulins Kill.. Wallpack.

Trout Run; village in Gloucester Township, Camden County, on Camden and Atlantic R. R............................. Mount Holly.

Tub Mill Branch; small brook in Bass River Township, Burlington County; flows into Wading River. { Mullica. / Little Egg Harbor.

Tuckahoe; river rising in southern part of Buena Vista Township; flows south, forming boundary between Maurice River and Weymouth townships, then southeast, forming boundary between Weymouth and Upper townships, into Great Egg Harbor. { Tuckahoe. / Great Egg Harbor.

Tucker; beach along coast of Little Egg Harbor Township, Burlington County...................................... Little Egg Harbor.

Tucker; island in Little Egg Harbor, in Little Egg Harbor Township, Burlington County .... Little Egg Harbor.

Tucker Beach; light on Tucker Beach, Little Egg Harbor Township, Burlington County .... Litt's Egg Harbor.

Tuckerton; creek in Little Egg Harbor Township, Burlington County; formed by the union of Shord Mill Brook and Gifford Mill Branch and flows into Little Egg Harbor... Little Egg Harbor.

Tuckerton; village in Little Egg Harbor Township, Burlington County, on Tuckerton R. R............................. Little Egg Harbor.

Tuft; point of land projecting from eastern coast of Woodbridge Township, Middlesex County, into Arthur Kill... Staten Island.

Tulepehauken; brook in Randolph Township, Burlington County; flows into West Branch of Wading River....... Mullica.

Tumble; village in southwestern part of Kingwood Township, Hunterdon County, on Delaware River and on Belvidere division Pennsylvania R. R .... Doylestown.

Tune Branch; brook in Brick Township, Ocean County; flows into Kettle Creek...................................... Asbury Park.

Turkey; brook in southern part of Mount Olive Township, Morris County; tributary to South Branch of Raritan River.. Lake Hopatcong.

Turkey; point of dry land projecting into the Glades in Downe Township, Cumberland County................... Bridgeton.

Turkey; village in Howell Township, Monmouth County ... Cassville.

Turner's Fork; brook in Lower Alloways Creek Township, Salem County; flows into Terrapin Gut .... Bayside.

Turnersville; village in Gloucester Township, Camden County; on South Branch of Timber Creek .... Philadelphia.

Turpentine; village in East Hampton Township, Burlington County.. Burlington.

Turtle; creek in Randolph Township, Burlington County; flows into Swan Bay...................................... Mullica.

Turtle; cove projecting from Manahawken Bay into Stafford Township, Ocean County................................ Long Beach.

Turtle; cove projecting from Reed Bay into Galloway Township, Atlantic County...................................... Atlantic City.

Turtle; pond in southeastern part of Green Township, Sussex County... Hackettstown.

Names of sheets.

Turtle Gut; life-saving station on southeastern coast of Lower Township, Cape May County......................... Cape May.

Turtle Gut; inlet projecting from Atlantic Ocean into southeastern shore of Lower Township, Cape May County .... Cape May.

Turtle Gut; passage in coast swamp in Middle Township, Cape May County... Dennisville.

Tuttle Corner; village in south central part of Sandyston Township, Sussex County.................................... Wallpack.

Tweed; creek in Fairfield Township, Cumberland County; flows into Back Creek .... Bayside.

Twilight; lake in Brick Township, Ocean County............ Asbury Park.

Two Bridges; village in southern part of Hardyston Township, on New York, Susquehanna and Western R. R., Sussex County .... Franklin.

Two Bridges; village in southeastern part of Pequannock Township, Morris County, at junction of Pompton and Passaic rivers..................................... Morristown.

Two Mile; beach on southeastern coast of Lower Township, Cape May County.. Cape May.

Two-penny Run; brook in Pilesgrove, Old Mans and Upper Penns Neck townships; flows into Game Creek, Salem County .... Salem.

Tyler Park; village in southern part of North Bergen Township, Hudson County, on New York, Susquehanna and Western R. R., and on Northern R. R. of New Jersey.... Paterson.

Uncle Tom; village in Egg Harbor Township, Atlantic County .... Great Egg Harbor.

Undercliffe; village in Orvil Township, Bergen County ..... Paterson.

Union; county in northeastern part of the State; area, 105 square miles. { Staten Island. / Plainfield.

Union; town in northeastern part of Hudson County........ Paterson.

Union; township in Bergen County; area, 10 square miles.. Paterson.

Union; township in Hudson County; area, 1 square mile.... Paterson.

Union; township in Hunterdon County; area, 20 square miles. Easton High Bridge.

Union; township in Ocean County; area, 45 square miles... { Whitings. / Long Beach. / Barnegat. / Little Egg Harbor.

Union; township in Union County; area, 15 square miles... { Staten Island. / Plainfield.

Union; village in western part of East Amwell Township, Hunterdon County..................................... Lambertville.

Union; village in Raritan Township, Monmouth County..... Sandy Hook.

Union; village in southern part of Rockaway Township, Morris County, on Den Brook............................. Lake Hopatcong.

Union; village in Union Township, Union County, on West Branch of Elizabeth River............................. Plainfield.

Union; village in northeastern part of Warren Township, Somerset County.. Plainfield.

Union Branch; brook in Manchester and Dover townships, Ocean County, tributary to Toms River. { Asbury Park. / Cassville. / Barnegat.

Union Clay Works; village in Lacey Township, Ocean County .... Whitings.

Names of sheets

Union Grove; village in Pittsgrove Township, Salem County. Glassboro.

Union Mills; village in Mount Laurel Township, Burlington County, on Mason Creek................................. Mount Holly.

Union Valley; village in Monroe Township, Middlesex County .... New Brunswick.

Unionville; village in southeastern part of Washington Township, Morris County.. Hackettstown.

Unionville; village in Galloway Township, Atlantic County. Mullica.

Upland Thorofare; passage in coast swamp in Upper Township, Cape May County.................................. Sea Isle.

Upper; township in Cape May County; area, 79 square miles. ⎰ Tuckahoe. ⎱ Sea Isle. ⎰ Dennisville. ⎱ Great Egg Harbor.

Upper Branch; brook rising in Quinton Township, flows southwest through Lower Alloways Creek Township, tributary to Stow Creek. ⎰ Salem. ⎱ Bayside.

Upper Cape Island; creek in southern part of Lower Township, Cape May County .... Cape May.

Upper Freehold; township in Monmouth County; area, 48 square miles. ⎰ Cassville. ⎱ Bordentown.

Upper Longwood; village situated in eastern part of Jefferson Township, Morris County............................ Lake Hopatcong.

Upper Macoupin; village in central part of West Milford Township, Passaic County.................................. Greenwood Lake.

Upper Mill; village in Pemberton Township, Burlington County .... Pemberton.

Upper Montclair; village in northern part of Montclair Township, Essex County, on New York and Greenwood Lake R. R.. Paterson.

Upper Montvale; village in northern part of Washington Township, Bergen County.................................. Ramapo.

Upper Neck; village in Pittsgrove Township, Salem County. Glassboro.

Upper Penns Neck; township in Salem County; area, 19 square miles .... Salem.

Upper Pittsgrove; township in Salem County; area, 36 square miles. ⎰ Glassboro. ⎱ Salem.

Upper Powhatcong; mountain in Mansfield Township, Warren County .... Hackettstown.

Uttertown; village in western part of West Milford Township, Passaic County .... Greenwood Lake.

Valley; village in western part of Bethlehem Township, Hunterdon County, on New Jersey Central R. R............... Easton.

Vanatta Station; village in Roxbury Township, Morris County, on Morris Canal and on Chester Branch of Delaware, Lackawanna and Western R. R...................... Lake Hopatcong.

Vancampens; brook rising in Wallpack Township, Sussex County, flowing southwest into Warren County, emptying into Delaware River in western part of Pahaquarry Township. ⎰ Bushkill Falls. ⎱ Wallpack.

Vanderburg; village in Atlantic Township, Monmouth County. Sandy Hook.

Vanhiseville; village in Jackson Township, Ocean County. Cassville.

Vanliews Corners; village in central part of East Amwell Township, Hunterdon County........................... Lambertville.

Names of sheets.

Vansyckles; village in Wantage Township, Sussex County, on New York, Susquehanna and Western R. R............ Port Jervis.

Van Syckles; village in northern part of Union Township, Hunterdon County.. High Bridge.

Vernon; township in Sussex County; area, 69 square miles. { Greenwood Lake. Goshen. Franklin. Port Jervis.

Vernon; village in central part of Vernon Township, Sussex County.. Greenwood Lake.

Verona; village in southeastern part of Caldwell Township. Essex County, on Peckman Brook........................ Paterson.

Vienna; village in western part of Independence Township, Warren County, on Pequest River........................ Hackettstown.

Villa Park; village in Wall Township, Monmouth County, on New York and Long Branch R. R....................... Asbury Park.

Vincentown; town in Southampton Township, Burlington County, on Vincentown and Evanstown Branch R. R. and { Mount Holly. on South Branch of Rancocas Creek. Pemberton.

Vineland; borough in Cumberland County................... Bridgeton.

Vliettown; village in western part of Bedminster Township, Somerset County, on Lamington River.................... Somerville.

Vol Sedge; islands in Union Township, Ocean County, in Barnegat Bay.. Long Beach.

Voorhees; village in eastern part of Franklin Township, Somerset County, on Mill Branch, Pennsylvania R. R.... New Brunswick.

Wading; river heading in two branches, the Oswego River, or East Branch, and the West Branch; flowing southeast { Pemberton. forms boundary between Bass River and Randolph town- Mullica. ships, Burlington County, emptying into Mullica River. Little Egg Harbor.

Wading Thorofare; passage in coast swamp in Galloway Township, Atlantic County .... Atlantic City.

Waldwick; village in Orvil Township, Bergen County ..... Ramapo.

Wall; small pond in southeastern part of Maurice River Township, Cumberland County .... Tuckahoe.

Wall; township in Monmouth County; area, 41 square miles. { Sandy Hook. Asbury Park.

Wallace Corner; village in southwestern part of West Milford Township, Passaic County, on Pequannock River and on New York, Susquehanna and Western R. R .... Greenwood Lake.

Wallkill; river heading in Byram Township, Sussex County, flowing north through Sparta and Hardyston Townships, and forms boundary between Wantage and Vernon townships; thence passing into New York, intersecting Orange and Ulster counties, and uniting with Rondout River about 6 miles from Hudson River, of which the Rondout is a tributary .... Franklin.

Wallpack; bend of Delaware River around southwest coast Wallpack Township, Sussex County .... Wallpack.

Wallpack; township in Sussex County; area, 23 square miles. Wallpack.

Wallpack Center; village in northern part of Wallpack Township, Sussex County............................... Wallpack.

Walnford; village in Upper Freehold Township, Monmouth County, on Crosswick Creek .... Bordentown.

A GEOGRAPHIC DICTIONARY OF NEW JERSEY. **123**

Names of sheets.

Walnut; brook in Raritan Township, Hunterdon County, tributary to Meshanic River. — High Bridge. Lambertville.

Walnut Valley; village in western part of Blairstown Township, Warren County — Delaware Water Gap.

Wanaque; village in southern part of Pompton Township, Passaic County, on Wanaque River and on New York and Greenwood Lake R. R. — Greenwood Lake.

Wanaque; river heading in Greenwood Lake, West Milford Township, Passaic County. It joins the Pequannock River at Pompton and together they form the Pompton River. — Morristown. Greenwood Lake.

Wantage; township in Sussex County; area, 68 square miles. — Port Jervis. Franklin.

Wardell Neck; point of land extending into Metedeconk River, in Brick Township, Ocean County — Asbury Park.

Ware Thorofare; passage in coast swamp in Dennis Township, Cape May County — Sea Isle.

Waretown; creek in Ocean Township, Ocean County; flows into Barnegat Bay — Barnegat.

Waretown; village in Ocean Township, on New Jersey Southern R. R., in Ocean County — Barnegat.

Waretown Station; village in Ocean Township, Ocean County — Barnegat.

Warford; creek in Kingwood Township, Hunterdon County; tributary to Delaware River — Doylestown.

Warne; brook in Madison Township, Middlesex County; flows into Tennent Brook — New Brunswick.

Warren; county in northwestern part of State on Delaware River; area, 365 square miles. — Bushkill Falls. Wallpack. Hackettstown. High Bridge. Delaware Water Gap. Easton.

Warren; township in Somerset County; area, 19 square miles. — Plainfield. Somerville.

Warrenville; village in south central part Allamuchy Township, Warren County — Hackettstown.

Warrenville; village in eastern part of Warren Township, Somerset County — Plainfield.

Warrington; village in central part of Knowlton Township, Warren County, on Paulins Kill and on New York, Susquehanna and Western R. R. — Delaware Water Gap.

Washington; borough in central part Washington Township, Warren County, on Morris Canal, at junction of Delaware, Lackawanna and Western R. R. with its Morris and Essex Division — Hackettstown.

Washington; town in northeastern part of East Brunswick Township, Middlesex County, on South River — New Brunswick.

Washington; township in Bergen County; area, 24 square miles. — Harlem. Tarrytown. Ramapo. Paterson.

Washington; township in Burlington County; area, 42 square miles — Mullica.

Names of sheets.

Washington; township in Gloucester County; area, 23 square miles. { Philadelphia. Glassboro. }

Washington; township in Mercer County; area, 21 square miles. { Princeton. Bordentown. }

Washington; township in Morris County; area, 45 square miles. { Lake Hopatcong. Hackettstown. High Bridge. Somerville. }

Washington; township in Warren County; area, 18 square miles. { Delaware Water Gap. Hackettstown. High Bridge. Easton. }

Washington; valley in Bridgewater and Warren townships, Somerset County. { Plainfield. Somerville. }

Washington; village in northwestern part of Green Township, Sussex County............................ Hackettstown.

Washington; village on boundary line between Randolph and Washington townships, Burlington County......... Mullica.

Washington Corner; village in southeastern part of Mendham Township, Morris County...................... Lake Hopatcong.

Washington Crossing; village in western part of Hopewell Township, Mercer County, on Delaware River and on Delaware and Raritan Canal and Belvidere Division, Pennsylvania R. R............................ Lambertville.

Washington Place; village in southwestern part of Livingston Township, Essex County.................... Morristown.

Washington Valley; village in western part Morris Township, Morris County............................ Lake Hopatcong.

Washingtonville; village in eastern part Hampton Township, Sussex County, on Paulins Kill and on New York, Susquehanna and Western R. R. { Wallpack. Franklin. }

Washingtonville; village in North Plainfield Township, Somerset County, on Stony Brook...................... Plainfield.

Watchung; village in Montclair Township, Essex County, on New York and Greenwood Lake R. R................ Paterson.

Waterford; township in Camden County; area, 57 square miles. { Mount Holly. Mullica. Hammonton. }

Waterford; village in Winslow Township, Camden County, on Camden and Atlantic R. R................... Hammonton.

Watering Place Branch; brook in Brick Township, Ocean County; flows into Lake Corasaljo.................. Asbury Park.

Watering Race; brook in Hamilton Township, Atlantic County; flows into Babcock Creek. { Mullica. Great Egg Harbor. }

Waterloo; village in southwestern part of Byram Township, Sussex County, on the boundary extending into Mount Olive Township, Morris County, on Morris Canal, Musconetcong River, and Delaware, Lackawanna and Western R. R............................ Hackettstown

Watsessing; village in southern part of Bloomfield Township, Essex County, on the Bloomfield Branch of Delaware, Lackawanna and Western R. R., where it crosses the Orange Branch of New York and Greenwood Lake R. R. Paterson.

Watson; creek in Wall Township, Monmouth County...... Asbury Park.

Names of sheets.

Waverly; village in southeastern part Clinton Township, Essex County, on Pennsylvania R. R .... Staten Island.

Wawayanda; lake in eastern part of Vernon Township, Sussex County.. Greenwood Lake.

Wawayanda; mountain range extending through entire central part of Vernon Township, Sussex County............. Greenwood Lake.

Wawayanda; village in eastern part of Vernon Township, Sussex County... Greenwood Lake.

Waycake; creek in Middletown, Holmdel and Raritan townships, Monmouth County; flows into Raritan Bay... Sandy Hook.

Waycake; lighthouse on south shore of Raritan Bay........ Sandy Hook.

Wayne; township in Passaic County; area, 27 square miles. { Paterson. Morristown. Greenwood Lake.

Wayne; village in western part of Wayne Township, Passaic County; on Morris Canal and on New York and Greenwood Lake R. R .... Morristown.

Weakfish Creek; passage in coast swamp in Upper Township, Cape May County .... Sea Isle.

Weasel; brook in Aquackanonck Township, Passaic County; passes through Passaic City and empties into Passaic River... Paterson.

Webb Mill; village in Lacey Township, Ocean County, on Webb Mill Branch... Whitings.

Webb Mill Branch; brook in Lacey Township, Ocean County; tributary to Chamberlain or Middle Branch............. Whitings.

Weehawken; township in Hudson County; area, 1 square mile .... Paterson.

Weekstown; village in Mullica Township, Atlantic County. Mullica.

Welchville; village in Mannington Township, Salem County. Salem.

Weldon; brook rising in western part of Jefferson Township, Morris County; it flows southwesterly into Lake Hopatcong in southwestern part of same township. } Franklin. Lake Hopatcong.

Well; island in Little Egg Harbor Township, Burlington County .... Little Egg Harbor.

Well Mills; village in Lacey Township, Ocean County..... Whitings.

Wellwood Station; part of Merchantville Borough, Camden County, on Amboy Division of Pennsylvania R. R....... Philadelphia.

Wemrock; brook in Freehold and Manalapan townships, Monmouth County; flows into Matchaponix Brook....... New Brunswick.

Wenonah; borough in Deptford Township, Gloucester County, on Mantua Creek and on West Jersey R. R .... Philadelphia.

Wertsville; village in eastern part East Amwell Township, Hunterdon County.. Lambertville.

Wescoatville; village in Mullica Township, Atlantic County. Mullica.

Wescott Mills; village in Monroe Township, Middlesex County, on Millstone River .... New Brunswick.

Wescottville; village in Deptford Township, Gloucester County.. Philadelphia.

Wesickaman; creek in Shamong Township, Burlington County, flows into Mullica or Atsion River. { Mullica. Pemberton.

West; brook in West Milford and Pompton townships, Passaic County, tributary to Wanaque River................ Greenwood Lake.

Names of sheets.

West Amwell; township in Hunterdon County; area, 20 square miles... Lambertville.

West Bergen; part of Jersey City, on Hackensack River and on Newark and New York R. R............................ Staten Island.

West Branch; brook in Hopewell Township, Cumberland County, flows into Cohansey Creek .... Salem.

West Branch; brook tributary to Wading River, in Randolph Township, Burlington County............................ Mullica.

West Branch of Papakating Creek; rises in western part of Wantage Township, flows in a southeasterly direction, and empties into Papakating Creek, in southern part of same township, Sussex County............................ Franklin.

West Cape May; borough in southwestern part of Cape May County... Cape May.

West Creek; village in western part of Dennis Township, Cape May County... Dennisville.

West Creek; village in Little Egg Harbor Township, Burlington County .... Little Egg Harbor.

West Creek Landing; village in northwestern part of Dennis Township, Cape May County, on West Creek........ Dennisville.

West Deptford; township in Gloucester County; area, 20 square miles .... Philadelphia.

West End; village in western part of Bethlehem Township, Hunterdon County, on Lehigh Valley R. R............... Easton.

West End; village in Ocean Township, Monmouth County, at junction of two branches of New York and Long Branch R. R... Sandy Hook.

West Englewood; village in western part of Englewood Township, Bergen County, on West Shore R. R........... Paterson.

West Farm; village in Howell Township, Monmouth County. Asbury Park.

West Freehold; village in Freehold Township, Monmouth County .... Cassville.

West Hampton; township in Burlington County; area, 11 square miles. { Burlington. Mount Holly.

West Hoboken; township in Hudson County; area, 1 square mile .... Paterson.

West Jersey Cranberry Meadow; marsh in Medford and Shamong townships, Burlington County, and Waterford Township, Camden County................................. Mount Holly.

West Livingston; village in southwestern part of Livingston Township, Essex County............................ Morristown.

West Milford; township in Passaic County; area, 80 square miles .... Greenwood Lake.

West Milford; village in central part of West Milford Township, Passaic County................................. Greenwood Lake.

West Orange; township in Essex County; area, 12 square miles. { Paterson. Morristown.

West Rutherford; village in northern part Union Township, and partly in Boiling Springs Township, Bergen County, on Passaic River and on New York, Lake Erie and Western R. R... Paterson.

West Summit; village in northeastern part New Providence Township, Union County, on Passaic and Delaware R. R. Plainfield.

West Windsor; township in Mercer County; area, 26 square miles. { Princeton. Bordentown.

Names of sheets.

Westecunk; creek in Little Egg Harbor Township, Burlington County, and Eagleswood Township, Ocean County; flows into Little Egg Harbor............................ Little Egg Harbor.

Westfield; township in Union County; area, 11 square miles. Plainfield.

Westfield; village in Westfield Township, Union County, on Central R. R. of New York............................ Plainfield.

Westmont Station; village in southeastern part of Haddon Township, Camden County, on Camden and Atlantic R. R. Philadelphia.

Weston; village in northwestern part of Franklin Township, Somerset County, on Millstone River and on Delaware and Raritan Canal............................ Somerville.

Westville; village in southwestern part of Caldwell Township, Essex County............................ Morristown.

Westville; village in West Deptford Township, Gloucester County, on Big Timber Creek and on West Jersey R. R... Philadelphia.

Westwood; village in southern part of Washington Township, Bergen County, on Pascack Creek and on New Jersey and New York R. R .... Paterson.

Weymouth; township in Atlantic County; area, 76 square miles. { Tuckahoe. { Great Egg Harbor.

Weymouth; village in Hamilton Township, Atlantic County, on Great Egg Harbor River............................ Hammonton.

Whale; creek in Matawan Township, Monmouth County, flowing into Raritan Bay............................ Sandy Hook.

Whale Pond; a continuation of Cranberry Brook, forming boundary between Eatontown and Ocean townships, Monmouth County, flows into Atlantic Ocean............................ Sandy Hook.

Wheat Road; station on New Jersey Southern R. R., in Buena Vista Township, Atlantic County............................ Hammonton.

Wheatland; village in Manchester Township, Ocean County, on New Jersey Southern R. R .... Whitings.

Wheatsheaf; village in western part of Linden Township, Union County .... Plainfield.

Whig Lane; village in Upper Pittsgrove Township, Salem County .... Glassboro.

Whippany; river rising in Mendham Township; flowing east through Morris and Hanover townships and emptying into Rockaway River near where it joins the Passaic River, in Morris County. { Morristown. { Lake Hopatcong.

Whippany; town in southern central part of Hanover Township, Morris County, on Whippany River............................ Morristown.

Whirlpool Channel; passage in coast swamp in Egg Harbor Township, Atlantic County .... Great Egg Harbor.

White; pond in southern part of Hardwick Township, Warren County. { Wallpack. { Hackettstown.

White; small pond in southwestern part of Andover Township, Sussex County .... Wallpack.

White; station in Dover Township, Ocean County, on New Jersey Southern R. R .... Cassville.

White Bridge; village in Bernard Township, Somerset County, on Passaic River. .... Somerville.

White Bridge; village in Jackson Township, Ocean County, on Toms River............................ Cassville.

White Creek; passage in coast swamp in Upper Township, Cape May County............................ Sea Isle,

Names of sheets.

White Horse; village in Hamilton Township, Mercer County. Bordentown.

White Horse; village in Woodland Township, Burlington County .... Pemberton.

White House; village in northern part of Readington Township, Hunterdon County, on Rockaway Creek and on Central R. R. of New Jersey .... High Bridge.

White Lake; small pond in northwestern part of Sparta Township, Sussex County.................................... Franklin.

White Marsh Run; brook in Millville Township, Cumberland County, flows into Maurice River .... Bridgeton.

White Meadow; small brook in western part of Rockaway Township, Morris County, tributary to Beaver Brook.... Lake Hopatcong.

White Oak; brook in Landis and Commercial townships, Cumberland County, flows into Manumuskin River...... Tuckahoe.

White Oak; island in swamp in Independence Township, Warren County... Hackettstown.

White Oak Bottom; village in Dover Township, Ocean County .... Asbury Park.

White Oak Branch; brook in Franklin and Monroe townships, Gloucester County, flows into Hospitality Branch of Great Egg Harbor River................................. Hammonton.

Whitesville; village in Neptune Township, Monmouth County.. Asbury Park.

Whitings; village in Manchester Township, Ocean County, on Philadelphia and Long Branch R. R................... Whitings.

Whitehall; village in southern part of Andover Township, Sussex County, on Sussex R. R.......................... Lake Hopatcong.

Whitehall; village in southern part of Lebanon Township, Hunterdon County... High Bridge.

Whitehall; brook in Franklin and Monroe townships, Gloucester County, flows into Hospitality Branch of Great Egg Harbor River. } Glassboro. Hammonton.

Whitehall; village in eastern part of Montville Township, Morris County, on Morris Canal, and on Boonton Branch of Delaware, Lackawanna and Western R. R .... Morristown.

Wickatunk; village in Marlboro Township, Monmouth County, on Freehold and New York R. R................. Sandy Hook.

Wickecheoke; creek in Raritan and Delaware townships, Hunterdon County, tributary to Delaware River........ Lambertville.

Wigwam; brook in Montclair and West Orange townships, Essex County, tributary to Second River.............. Paterson.

Wilburtha; village in Ewing Township, Mercer County, on Delaware River, on Delaware and Raritan Canal, and on Belvidere Division of the Pennsylvania R. R.......... Lambertville.

Wild Cat Branch; brook in Waterford Township, Camden County, flows into Mechesactauxin Branch of Mullica River.. Hammonton.

Wilkins; village in Medford Township, Burlington County, on Medford Branch, Pennsylvania R. R., Amboy Division.. Mount Holly.

Williams Mine; situated in southern part Vernon Township, Sussex County... Greenwood Lake.

Williamstown; village in Monroe Township, Gloucester County, on Philadelphia and Reading R. R .... Hammonton.

Names of sheets.

Wiliamstown Junction; village at junction of Philadelphia and Reading R. R., and Philadelphia and Atlantic City R. R., in Winslow Township, Camden County. — Mount Holly. Hammonton.

Willingboro; township in Burlington County; area. 7 square miles .... — Burlington.

Willis Run; brook rising in northern part of Dennis Township, Cape May County, flowing southwest into East Creek. — Dennisville

Willis Thorofare; passage in swamp in southeastern part Upper Township, Cape May County .... — Great Egg Harbor.

Willitt Thorofare; passage in coast swamp in Little Egg Harbor Township, in Burlington County .... — Little Egg Harbor.

Willoughby; brook in western part of High Bridge Township, Hunterdon County, tributary to Spruce Run ...... — High Bridge.

Willow; brook tributary to Hop Brook, forms partial boundary between Holmdel Township and Atlantic and Marlboro townships, Monmouth County...................... — Sandy Hook.

Willow Grove; village in southeastern part Fanwood Township, Union County....................................... — Plainfield.

Willow Grove; village in Landis Township, Cumberland County .... — Glassboro.

Wilson; landing in Hamilton Township, Atlantic County, on Gravelly Run .... — Great Egg Harbor.

Wilson; village in Chester Township, Burlington County, on Pennsylvania R. R.. — Mount Holly.

Wilton; village in Winslow Township, Camden County..... — Mount Holly.

Winslow; township in Camden County; area, 59 square miles. — Hammonton. Mount Holly. Glassboro.

Winslow; village in Winslow Township, Camden County, on New Jersey Southern R. R............................... — Hammonton.

Winslow Junction; village in Winslow Township, Camden County .... — Hammonton.

Windsor; village in Washington Township, Mercer County, on Pennsylvania R. R., Amboy Division.................. — Bordentown.

Wolf Run; brook in Bass River Township, Burlington County, flows into Bass River..................................... — Little Egg Harbor.

Wood; swamp in Plumstead Township, Ocean County...... — Cassville.

Woodbine; village in northern part of Dennis Township, Cape May County, on West Jersey R. R.................. — Dennisville.

Woodbourne; village in south central part of Wantage Township, on Western Branch of Papakating Creek, in Sussex County .... — Franklin.

Woodbridge; creek in Woodbridge Township, Middlesex County, tributary to Arthur Kill......................... — Plainfield.

Woodbridge; township in Middlesex County; area, 30 square miles. — Staten Island. Plainfield.

Woodbridge; village in central part of Woodbridge Township, Middlesex County, on Heard Brook, and on Perth Amboy Branch, Pennsylvania R. R .... — Plainfield.

Woodbury; city in Gloucester County, on Woodbury Creek, and at junction of three branches of West Jersey R. R.; area, 2 square miles .... — Philadelphia.

Woodbury; creek rises in Deptford Township, Gloucester County, flows through West Deptford Township, and thence empties into Delaware River.................... — Philadelphia.

130   A GEOGRAPHIC DICTIONARY OF NEW JERSEY.

Names of sheets.

Woodcliff; village in central part of Washington Township, Bergen County, on Pascack Creek, and on New Jersey and New York R. R .... Ramapo.

Woodfern; village in southwestern part of Branchburg Township, Somerset County, on South Branch of Raritan River, on South Branch R. R., and on Lehigh Valley R. R ...... High Bridge.

Woodland; township in Burlington County; area, 117 square miles. { Whitings. Pemberton. }

Woodmansie; village in Woodland Township, Burlington County, on New Jersey Southern R. R .... Whitings.

Woodport; village in western part of Jefferson Township, Morris County, on Lake Hopatcong .... Lake Hopatcong.

Woodridge; town in western part Lodi Township, Bergen County, on New Jersey and New York R. R .... Paterson.

Woodruff; village in Deerfield Township, Cumberland County, on New Jersey Southern R. R .... Bridgeton.

Woodruff; village in Plumstead Township, Ocean County .. Cassville.

Woodruff; creek in Elizabeth Township, Union County, tributary to Bound Creek .... Staten Island.

Woodruff Gap; village in northwestern part Sparta Township, on Lehigh and Hudson River R. R., Sussex County.. Franklin.

Woodside; village, part of Newark City, Essex County, on Passaic River, and on Paterson and Newark Branch of New York, Lake Erie and Western R. R................. Paterson.

Woodside Park; village, part of Newark City, Essex County, on Second River, at junction of Orange Branch of New York and Greenwood Lake R. R. with New York and Greenwood Lake R. R .... Paterson.

Woodstown; borough in Salem County..................... Salem.

Woodsville; village in northern part of Hopewell Township, Mercer County... Lambertville.

Woolsey; brook in Hopewell Township, Mercer County, tributary to Jacobs Creek............................... Lambertville.

Woolwich; township in Gloucester County; area, 22 square miles .... Salem.

Wortendyke; village in eastern part of Franklin Township, Bergen County, on New York, Susquehanna and Western R. R... Paterson.

Wrangel; brook in Manchester and Berkley townships, Ocean County, tributary to Toms River. { Barnegat. Whitings. }

Wreck; pond in Wall Township, Monmouth County, flows into Sea Island Inlet.................................... Asbury Park.

Wrights; small pond in central part Byram Township, Sussex County .... Lake Hopatcong.

Wrightstown; village in New Hanover Township, Burlington County, on Pemberton and Hightstown R. R......... Bordentown.

Wrightsville; village in Upper Freehold Township, Monmouth County .... Bordentown.

Wyckoff; village in central part Franklin Township, Bergen County, on New York, Susquehanna and Western R. R. .. Ramapo.

Wykertown; village in eastern part Frankford Township, Sussex County... Franklin.

Wyoming; village in Millburn Township, Essex County, on Delaware, Lackawanna and Western R. R............... Plainfield.

Names of sheets.

Yantecaw; river rising in eastern part Essex County, flows through Franklin Township same county, and across southeastern part Acquackanonck Township, Passaic County, into Passaic River............................. Paterson.

Yard; creek in western part Blairstown Township, Warren County, flows southwest into Paulins Kill in central part of Knowlton Township .... Delaware Water Gap.

Yard; creek rising in Catfish Pond, Pahaquarry Township, { Bushkill Falls.
Warren County, empties into Paulins Kill at Harrisburg. { Delaware Water Gap.

Yardville; village in Hamilton Township, Mercer County, on Doctor Creek.. Bordentown.

Yellow; brook in Howell and Atlantic townships, Monmouth County, tributary to Swimming River............. Sandy Hook.

Yellow Brook; village in Howell Township, Monmouth County .... Asbury Park.

Young; island in swamp in Independence Township, Warren County.. Hackettstown.

Youngstown; village in Randolph Township, Morris County. Lake Hopatcong.

Yorktown; village in Pilesgrove Township, Salem County.. Salem.

Zebs Bridge; village in Berkeley Township, Ocean County, on Davenport Branch .... Whitings.